100

THINGS TO DO IN

RALEIGH

BEFORE YOU

DIE

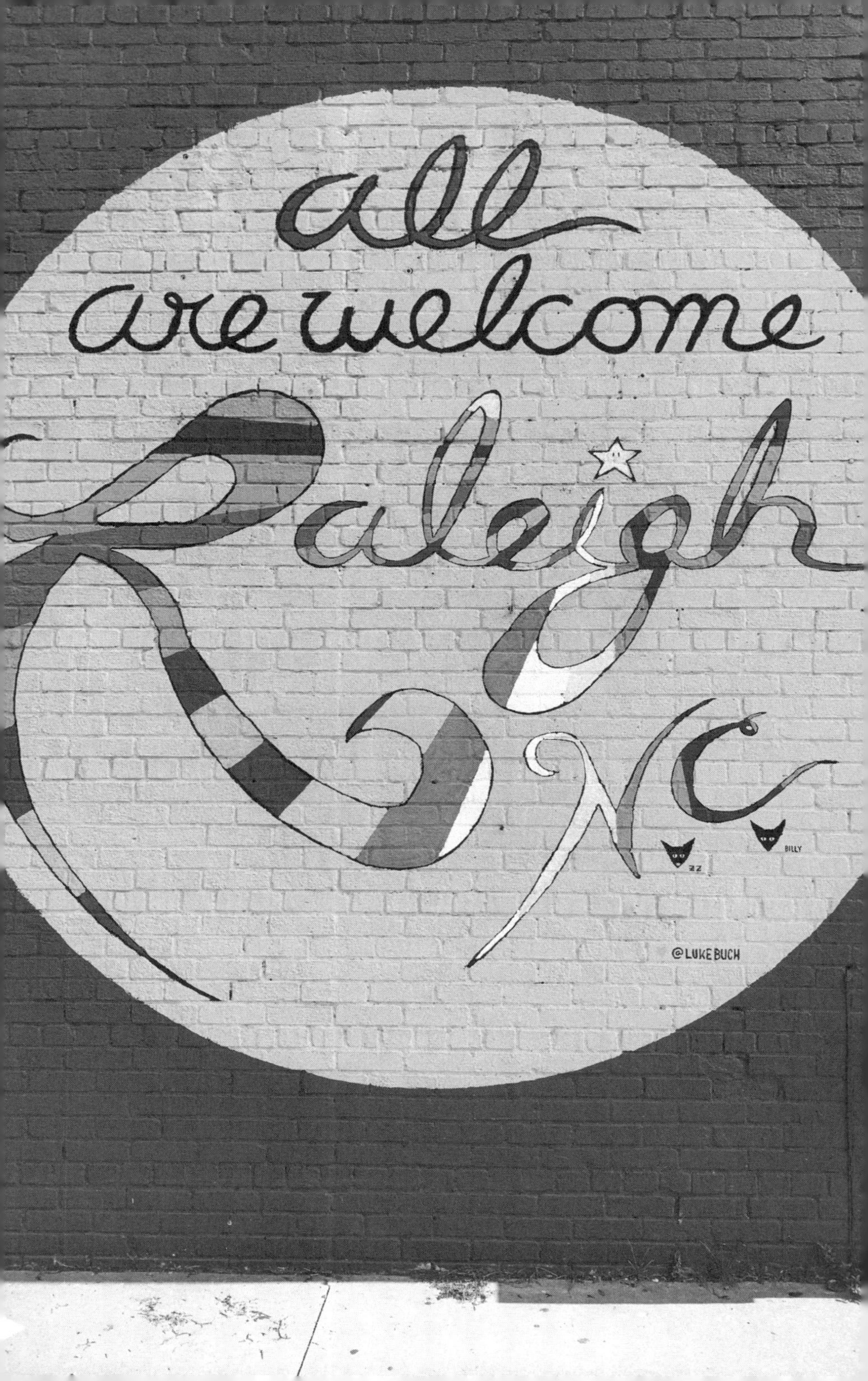
all
are welcome
Raleigh
NC
ZZ
BILLY
@LUKEBUCH

100

THINGS TO DO IN

RALEIGH
BEFORE YOU
DIE

• •

ALLI HURLEY

REEDY PRESS

Library of Congress Control Number: 2021948916

ISBN: 9781681063515

Design by Jill Halpin

All photos by the author unless otherwise noted.

Printed in the United States of America
22 23 24 25 26   5 4 3 2 1

DEDICATION

For Graham

· ·

CONTENTS

Music and Entertainment

Sports and Recreation

Shopping and Fashion

PREFACE

Raleigh has the disarming distinction of being an innovative incubator while never sacrificing charming, hometown spirit. All across the map are cities cranking out success stories of grandeur. Raleigh manages the same, all the while never wavering as a genuinely gratifying place to live. People come, create opportunity, and stay. It's a city of the deliberate and the friendly. In the sweet spot between the mountains and the sea (attention, day trippers!), it's bursting with free public programming, invigorating private enterprise, and a grassroots enthusiasm you just can't contrive. Our City of Oaks is indeed an exceptionally well-kept secret. While the entries in this guide were chosen (among hordes of other, very worthy candidates) for novelty, memorability, quality, and public admiration, the tipping point for inclusion was that they all have something quintessentially "Raleigh" about them. They are entrepreneurial, community-oriented, authentic. Raleigh is all about big-league opportunity with small-town camaraderie, so grab your pals, stomp the yard, and fall in love with our lush oasis.

ACKNOWLEDGMENTS

Thank you to the people of Raleigh, who cherish the spirit of our city and choose to invest in its well-being.

FOOD AND DRINK

PAY IT FORWARD,
PAY WHAT YOU'RE ABLE, OR
VOLUNTEER AT A PLACE AT THE TABLE

This charming and socially invigorating nonprofit café is Raleigh's first and only pay-what-you-can restaurant. A frequent volunteer at neighborhood soup kitchens in her youth, Maggie Kane, founder of A Place at the Table (APATT), emphasizes in her 2020 TED Talk the need for dignity, community, and choice, regardless of monetary means. She envisioned and launched APATT, where patrons can pay a "suggested price," pay less, pay more, or volunteer for their meals. It's a reimagined concept of the traditional soup kitchen, one where there is a refreshing lack of division between those who can pay and those who can't. The breakfast and lunch menus, curated thoughtfully from seasonal ingredients, are classic, filling, and decidedly not-fussy, but steeped in freshness and hit-the-spot flavor.

300 W Hargett St., #50, (919) 307-8914
tableraleigh.org

TIP
Head across the street for a picnic in Nash Square and meet your newest friend, Berkeley, a gigantic, wood-carved squirrel and former legendary Raleigh oak tree that had succumbed to disease.

CELEBRATE ALL OCCASIONS
AND IMMERSE IN NORTH CAROLINA CULTURE AT ANGUS BARN

Purveyor of buttery steaks, host of all occasions worth celebrating, and pillar of the Raleigh spirit, Angus Barn—literally a giant, red barn—is a storied Raleigh landmark. More than a restaurant, it's a veritable museum of decor, as owner Van Eure has collected thousands of antique pieces from across the state. All the dining rooms feel at once exciting and homey, but arguably the most intriguing is the Wild Turkey Bar and Lounge, thanks to hundreds of decorative, turkey-shaped decanters. With its well-stocked wine cellar, drool-worthy steaks, singular hospitality, and commitment to environmental stewardship, Angus Barn is, in a word, inspiring. Look out for Eure as she weaves through the restaurant, greeting every guest like a long-lost friend.

9401 Glenwood Ave., (919) 781-2444
angusbarn.com

TIP
Decorations and lights come early and stay late during the holidays at Angus Barn. They are widely regarded as some of the most festive in the area.

FIND DOWN-HOME COMFORT
AND BIG-TIME PANCAKE COMPETITION
AT BIG ED'S

Through and through a family business, there are now three Big Ed's in the area. Step inside to checkered tablecloths, the warm aroma of Southern comfort, and in the case of the City Market spot, antique farm equipment hanging from the ceiling. Choose from familiar favorites like ham and gravy or steak and eggs, served with tried-and-true staples like Grandmother's Mac 'n' Cheese, the recipe literally handed down through the generations. Hungry for some healthy competition? Enter the Pancake Challenge! Gobble down three plate-sized flapjacks in 45 minutes or fewer and snag a free T-shirt prize! The lunch menu is handwritten daily and crowned with a blue-plate special, the best bang for your buck.

City Market
220 Wolfe St., (919) 836-9909

North
5009 Falls of Neuse Rd., (919) 747-9533

South
231 Timber Dr., Garner, (919) 900-7764

bigedsnc.com

TIP

Don't miss out on the homemade buttermilk biscuits, and be sure to pair them the Big Ed's way, with butter and blackstrap molasses.

HONE YOUR CRAFT
AT BREWGALOO

Crazy for craft beer? Make yourself right at home. Brewgaloo, posting up downtown over two days in September, has snagged top honors not once but twice in *USA Today*'s "10Best" as the best beer festival in the nation. Friday Night Block Party is sampler city. A smaller, more intimate event compared to Brewgaloo's Saturday Street Fest, the block party is ticketed admission but includes unlimited three-ounce tastings of barrel-aged and sour beers, exclusively available then and there. Saturday kicks the hype into high gear with live music, food trucks, local vendors, and of course mucho brew. The festival is free to enter on Saturday, but tickets are required to redeem for samplers and pints. If ales and IPAs don't float your boat, there are other inviting options, such as wine, cider, milkshakes, and smoothies.

(919) 755-9235
shoplocalraleigh.org/brewgaloo

TIP
Look out for discounted tickets available online, ahead of time, for both Friday Night Block Party and Saturday Street Fest.

GO GLUTEN-FREE
AT FOUNT COFFEE + KITCHEN

Four founders recognized a need for local, quality coffee and allergen-friendly refreshments in the Research Triangle Park area of Raleigh, and thus Fount was born. The diversity of its clientele (families, students, business professionals) points to a shop bent on inclusiveness. You'll find folks there to work, study, chat, read, or just enjoy the general camaraderie of the space. Coffee is sourced from Counter Culture, a local roaster just a few miles from Fount. Each month, it also features a domestic or international specialty roaster. On its 100 percent gluten-free menu, you'll find in-house baked goods, a variety of gluten-free toast stacks, smoothie bowls, salads, and small plates, all thoughtfully labeled with vegetarian, vegan, and dairy-free signage. To quote the founders, "Coffee is a universal language!"

10954 Chapel Hill Rd., Morrisville, (984) 888-5454
fountcoffee.com

TIP

Look for the specialty lattes, rotating seasonally, such as orange maple spice. Dairy-free options are available, and if caffeine isn't your thing, stop by in the afternoons for locally brewed beers and wines.

FEEL THE ASIAN-INSPIRED, SOUTHERN-LOVING FUSION
AT GARLAND

If ever there is an example of a multi-hyphenate powerhouse, it's Cheetie Kumar, local rockstar (literally), James Beard award nominee, and head chef and co-owner of Garland, where ingredients and flavors flawlessly reflect her artistic creativity. Nothing about the Asian-Indian fusion cuisine is typical, and yet that's what makes Garland a staple of Raleigh. Like Raleigh, Garland food celebrates international influence with a Southern twist. Locally sourced ingredients reflect the availability of the season, making the experience one of a kind. The "sharing plates" are a fun way to kick off the meal and sample a full spectrum of flavor combinations. The cocktails, also decidedly creative and scrumptious, are well worth ordering alongside Kumar's cooking. Icing on the proverbial cake are the ample gluten-free options.

14 W Martin St., (919) 833-6886
garlandraleigh.com

FALL BACK TO THE '40S
AT HAYES BARTON CAFÉ AND DESSERTERY

An upscale diner with down-home comfort food, this café has a knack for nostalgia. The walls are adorned with World War II memorabilia, from glamour shots to soldier portraits, along with a few cameos of young Elvis peppered in. Even the menu pays homage to the 1940s, with cleverly concocted film puns ("Quesa Blanca" to start, anyone?). It is nestled in the historic Five Points neighborhood; the decor is retro yet refreshing, the vibe quirky yet cozy, and the food sentimental yet stimulating. Whatever you do, don't skip dessert. Enormous pies and cakes perch cheerily in the display like pillars of decadence. Order by the slice, stay put or take away, and don't be shy about sharing: one slab can quench the cravings of two or three ravenous grownups.

2000 Fairview Rd., (919) 856-8551
hayesbartoncafeanddessertery.com

FRENCH IT UP
AT JOLIE

Everything about Jolie feels authentically French: the airy brightness, the blue accents, the chic yet understated decor, the romantic ambience. But these are all opening acts for the star of the show: food, magnifique food! Chef, owner, mastermind, and five-time James Beard award nominee Scott Crawford is a veritable celebrity around these parts, and rightfully so. On the rotating menu, look for familiar favorites like onion soup and steak frites so tender you can toss your knife (gently) aside. Among the classics, other dishes feature twists of innovation, such as his signature escargot presentation with baguette. While reservations are ideal for the downstairs dining room, the cozy kitchen bar is first-come, first-serve, as is "le rooftop," the divinely pleasant upstairs patio brimming with pots of fragrant herbs. Bon appétit!

620 N Person St., (919) 803-7221
restaurantjolie.com

TRY A BITE OF EVERYTHING
AT MORGAN STREET AND TRANSFER CO. FOOD HALLS

Lots of opinionated foodies in your posse? Morgan Street and Transfer Co. food halls have every edible option imaginable. Eateries and food retailers line both trendy warehouse spaces, with concepts inspired from far and wide, such as Thailand and Lebanon, and closer to home, such as New England and our own City of Oaks. The all-weather outdoor patio and bar is a smash hit at Morgan Street, featuring festive ambience effused from market lighting and lush greenery. Transfer Co. as well includes a popping patio with individual tables and cheery, yellow umbrellas. Coffee or cocktails, pizza or prime rib, empanadas or axe-throwing, it's all under one roof. Indeed, there is a dedicated stall at Morgan Street for safe and supervised axe-throwing (to work up an appetite, naturally).

Morgan Street Food Hall
411 W Morgan St., (919) 307-4481
morganfoodhall.com

Transfer Co. Food Hall
500 E Davie St., (984) 232-8122
transfercofoodhall.com

EXPERIENCE PASTRY PERFECTION
AT LucetteGrace

Just when you think a French macaron can't get more heavenly, LucetteGrace throws your sweet tooth a summer ice cream rendition and the angel choir reaches a fever pitch. *Merci beaucoup*. LucetteGrace is a celebration of patisserie and an unmatched purveyor of confectionery perfection in Raleigh. The menu rotates frequently, keeping pace with coming holidays, seasons, and celebrations, which happily gives you ample opportunity to frequent a tall, yellow stool by the window and snack on fresh flavors. Order classics like king cake for Mardi Gras, buche de Noel for Christmas, pink anything for Valentine's Day, and birthday cake macarons for, well, you know. Rounding out the menu are savory bites for breakfast and lunch, classic café beverages, and gluten-free offerings.

235 S Salisbury St., (919) 307-4950
lucettegrace.com

TIP

If you've ever wondered what the Eiffel Tower would look like in macaron form, LucetteGrace has filled in the blank. Its celebration menu offers for pre-order a literal tower of those charming French delights.

QUENCH YOUR 'CUE CRAVINGS
AT PEAK CITY PIG FEST

There are pit master barbecue competitions and there are lively food festivals. Peak City Pig Fest is both. Amen. You're going to want ample time at this free, two-day event in Historic Downtown Apex (just southwest of Raleigh). Approximately 40 teams are judged by a pre-selected panel to find the most masterful interpretations of barbecued chicken, ribs, brisket, and pork. There is also an "Anything Butt" category for all other varieties of delectable dishes except barbecue. Sanctioned by the Kansas City Barbecue Society and benefiting the Apex Sunrise Rotary Foundation, it's a draw for thousands who come to witness the steamy competition, drink beer, listen to all-day live music, and cash in on a divinely tasty helping of 'cue.

Downtown Apex, (919) 362-7141
peakcitypigfest.com

COME ONE, COME ALL
TO POOLE'S DINER

Ashley Christensen, her name around Raleigh (and beyond) synonymous with ingenious, is the chef/owner of Poole's, as well as five other local establishments. She's been an unequivocal leader of the food boom in Raleigh, receiving the James Beard Award for Outstanding Chef in 2019. Best of all, her cooking remains as Southern-comfort-inspired as ever. Step into Poole's for a winning marriage of premier yet approachable dining. The menu items are a rotating expression of what's locally and seasonally available. First and foremost, order the famous macaroni au gratin, a deep dish of creamy indulgence, baked for a crispy finish on top. You could share, but don't. To paraphrase Chef Ashley, come in a T-shirt or a tuxedo and make yourself at home.

426 S McDowell St., (919) 832-4477
ac-restaurants.com/pooles

TIP
Poole's is just a couple of blocks away from the Duke Energy Center for the Performing Arts, making it the perfect stop on the way to or from an evening show or matinee.

RELAX WITH THE RECORD-HOLDERS
AT RALEIGH BEER GARDEN

When your local bar holds the Guinness World Record for most beers on tap, you know you're in the right town. With three stories; expansive, greenery-clad rooftop and patio space; and approximately 365 selections of beer, all the way from international to craft, Raleigh Beer Garden is a tree-house haven of fermentation. To avoid the aches of analysis paralysis, opt for a flight of beer to test the waters (well, suds). The Garden also offers up a full dining menu with beer-complementing sustenance like burgers and pizza. As for the atmosphere, they mean business, I mean leisure, when they say "garden." Leafy greenery sprouts all over the establishment, and a 40-foot reconstructed pecan tree from Creedmoor, North Carolina, stands nobly front and center.

614 Glenwood Ave., (919) 324-3415
theraleighbeergarden.com

TIP
Bring your pup along to this fur-friendly establishment, and treat your pal with a snack from the "Hungry Dawgs" menu.

JOURNEY BACK TO YESTERYEAR
AT SECOND EMPIRE

The Dodd-Hinsdale House, a regal mansion on Hillsborough Street, was erected circa 1879 in the Second Empire Victorian fashion and was rescued over a century later from near-demolition to become a fine-dining, formal yet friendly, sincere but not stuffy, allergy-sensitive, one-of-a-kind Raleigh experience. Cocktails on the covered porch are a promising start before heading inside to full-fledged historical elegance, complete with opulent oil paintings and grandiose gilded mirrors. Food presentation is artistic and celebratory, with full-bodied flavor to match. Upscale yet affordable, globally inspired yet distinctly Southern, the cuisine is at once novel and familiar, like the house itself. This is your gateway to the disarming combination of history and hospitality. PS: They have gluten-free calamari. 'Nuff said.

330 Hillsborough St., (919) 829-3663
second-empire.com

TIP
Don't miss the Tavern, located downstairs in an exposed-brick cellar. It's an alternative way to experience Second Empire: quality food and service, but with informal dining and beer on tap.

DOWN
A DOZEN "HOT MINIS"
AT SOLA COFFEE CAFÉ

Sola is an embodiment of one of Raleigh's greatest strengths: emphasis on relationships. In addition to its cornucopia of fresh, brunch-centric fare like colorful breakfast bowls, seasonal salads, and comforting egg omelets and sammies, it draws in talent and expertise from other local artisans. The Sola experience is routinely rounded out by flower vendors, artists, and live musicians. The latte art at Sola very nearly breaks your heart to spoil, but even so, it would be heinous not to indulge. Quite possibly the most famed features of this family-owned, neighborhood operation are the "hot minis." Puffy, little clouds of sweet dough, they come out warm and fresh from the kitchen with your choice of topping and are more than acceptable to down by the dozen.

7705 Lead Mine Rd., (919) 803-8983
solacoffee.com

TIP

Take a moment to snap your pic in front of the legendary "I believe in Raleigh" mural to celebrate this sweet establishment and her hometown.

SAMPLE THE CITY
WITH A TASTE CAROLINA FOOD TOUR

Taste Carolina's walking food tour blazes a brilliant pathway to comb through the vibrant and eclectic offerings in Raleigh, whether you're a weekender keen to sample the scene or a lifelong resident keeping an ear to the street. With a knowledgeable guide at the helm, you'll storm the sidewalks of downtown, garnering snatches of history about our fair city along the way. You'll stop at approximately five or six independently owned establishments and sample a curated mix of small plates, cocktails, desserts, and other local provisions. The portion sizes are small enough to leave room for future stops but big enough to capture the concept. Since the participating restaurants change weekly, you've got the golden hall pass to keep tasting.

220 Fayetteville St., (919) 237-2254
tastecarolina.net

PEDAL OFF THE CARBS
WITH TROLLEY PUB TOUR

On any given night in downtown Raleigh, an open-air trolley is trundling up the streets, powered by the legs on board. It's eco-friendly, it's bumpin' the tunes, it's the Trolley Pub of Raleigh! This is your chance to pub crawl on wheels. You can rent out the whole trolley for private parties, events, and corporate outings, or snag a seat alongside other individuals for the "Mixer Tour" (see what they did there?). Safely strapped to their stools, with a driver and tour guide at the wheel, passengers begin pedaling, stationary-bike style, churning the Trolley Pub into motion. Over the course of a couple of hours, you'll sip and sing along, stopping at two to three downtown pubs or breweries and conveniently burning the carbs as you guzzle.

323 W Davie St., (919) 473-3312
trolleypub.com/raleigh

TIP

On a designer tour, you'll be able to BYOB on board the trolley (they provide an ice-stocked cooler), designate the tunes, and single out your pub stops along the way. Come prepared to call the shots (pardon me).

PEEK INSIDE THE BEAN-TO-BAR PROCESS
AT VIDERI CHOCOLATE FACTORY

Esse quam videri: to be rather than to seem. It's our state motto and the guiding principle behind Videri Chocolate Factory. Cruise by the outdoor pickup window for soft-serve ice cream, or step inside for a peek behind the confectionery curtain. Guests are invited to conduct self-guided, sample-laden tours through the factory, using helpful signage and descriptions of the bean-to-bar process. Afterward, sip a coffee from the café (frozen hot chocolate a must during summer), stock up on bars and bonbons, and enjoy the chocolate-infused ambience. Don't miss the private outdoor patio, a secluded, airy spot to indulge in the spoils of your visit. In the words of co-founder Sam Ratto, "The best way to compliment chocolate is to eat it."

327 W Davie St., (919) 755-5053
viderichocolatefactory.com

TIP

You can find Videri chocolate running rampant around Raleigh, in restaurants, grocery stores, and other retail spaces. A trusted favorite for locals, the ingredients are gluten-, soy-, egg-, and nut-free.

SINK INTO
THE CITY SKYLINE
AT WYE HILL

Wye Hill is high atop the list of best spots for Raleigh brews with a view. Just west of downtown, it's everything to love about our leafy little city: chef-curated fare, craft drinks, soul-restoring skyline views, and a patio that launches outdoor dining to new realms of pleasure. Food and drink are equally delicious here, so Wye Hill is an across-the-board hot spot for afternoon sips, sunset supper, or a late-evening snack. Even so, the showstopper may just be Sunday brunch. Diverse yet manageable, the brunch menu covers a full spectrum of sweet and savory, from French toast to shrimp and grits. Obviously, brunch wouldn't be complete without mimosas, which are seasonally inspired and mixed according to your specifications.

201 S Boylan Ave., (984) 200-1189
wyehill.com

STEP UNDERGROUND FOR SPEAKEASY SPLENDOR
AT WATTS & WARD

In a leather-appointed, bookshelf-adorned underground den beneath Hargett Street, cocktails flow and the Prohibition-era speakeasy lives on in full romanticism. Named for the North Carolina laws that forbade the sale of spirits over 100 years ago, Watts & Ward continues to propagate the lively speakeasy culture that buoyed the enthusiasm of liquor-loving renegades back in the day. In the vein of secrecy, you enter the lounge via an unassuming, street-level stairwell to the subterranean space below. Expansive and richly decorated, Watts & Ward has several bar counters throughout the cavern, with room upon vintage room to explore. On balmier evenings, enjoy drinks on the outdoor patio with full confidence that while the vibes are 1920s, the laws of Prohibition have happily come and gone.

200 S Blount St., (919) 896-8016
wattsandward.com

TIP

Begin your evening with dinner at Caffé Luna, a cozy Italian nook and well-loved Raleigh establishment located on the street corner just above Watts & Ward.

MUSIC
AND ENTERTAINMENT

REVEL IN ELEGANCE
AT CAROLINA BALLET

Right in our backyard are dancers capable of performing the most demanding feats of athleticism with effortless grace. Founded in 1997, Carolina Ballet company boasts wildly talented dancers from all over the world, many from right here in Raleigh. The ballet is a mesmerizing combination of music, sport, and beauty and is a unique way to reimagine storytelling in the absence of speech. While regular season performances typically take place in the intimate Fletcher Opera Theater (where you can literally see the muscles rippling), Carolina Ballet's annual rendition of *The Nutcracker* is reserved for Raleigh Memorial Auditorium and its crystal chandelier-clad, red-velvet embrace. In Raleigh at Christmastime, there are few events as nostalgic and stunning as Carolina Ballet taking the stage to Tchaikovsky's opening chords.

2 E South St., (919) 719-0800 (box office)
carolinaballet.com

SWOON OVER SMOOTH JAZZ
AT C. GRACE

A swoop of the saxophone, a pluck of the upright bass, a sultry piano rift, and you're sinking into the smooth jazz like it's a bathtub full of melted chocolate. A classic jazz club through and through, C. Grace is vintage and intimate and has the sizzling tunes and quality cocktails to go the distance. The focal point of the lounge is a velvet-draped stage, where seasoned musicians entertain the onlookers with alluring vocals and intricate instrumentation. On weekends, arrive early and sit close to the stage for an immersive experience. The low lighting and plush decor of the back room are ideal for a quiet drink, or maybe even a tarot card reading. From Tuesday through Saturday, heat up, simmer down, and get lost in a musical embrace.

407 Glenwood Ave., (919) 899-3675
cgracebar.com

TUNE IN FOR SUMMER TOURS AND TAILGATING
AT COASTAL CREDIT UNION MUSIC PARK AT WALNUT CREEK

This outdoor music pavilion has known a smattering of other titles since its genesis in 1991, but it is usually referred to locally as Walnut Creek Amphitheatre. With space for 20,000 strong, the venue hosts some of the biggest worldwide touring acts and has become a staple of Raleigh's summertime entertainment. Perched on the southeastern side of the city, Walnut Creek is your accessible escape to the country for good vibes only. While you can't bring food and beverages into the venue proper (excepting water), the parking lot has enormous pregame potential. Meet your friends, drop a tailgate, bring a picnic, and hype up (or wind down) before the show. Inside the venue, choose from reserved seating closer to the stage or general admission lawn seating, ideal for group gatherings.

3801 Rock Quarry Rd., (919) 831-6400
walnutcreekamphitheatre.com

RELAX WITH OLDIES, R&B, AND EVERYTHING IN BETWEEN
AT COASTAL CREDIT UNION MIDTOWN PARK

This lush, grassy amphitheater in the heart of North Hills has known many bare feet, fold-open chairs, and chill vibes. On Thursday evenings during the summer, come for low-key, outdoor concert-lovin' and bands cranking out oldies, R&B, beach tunes, and Motown (not all at the same time, of course). Surrounded by dozens of shops and restaurants, it's the perfect place to wind down after a day out and about. Transitioning into fall, the venue continues to host live music with a laid-back ambience on Friday nights with country, classic rock, reggae, and tribute bands. Check the lineup for your favorites and bring your chairs, bring your kids, bring your car, and park it for free in the attached deck.

4011 Cardinal Drive at North Hills Street, (919) 719-5442
visitnorthhills.com/events/page/2

JAM WITH J. COLE
AT DREAMVILLE FESTIVAL

It might be fair to say that platinum-certified, Grammy-winning musician J. Cole has seen some success. On top of his professional accomplishments, he also gives back generously and intentionally to his home state of North Carolina. One of Cole's philanthropic ventures is the Dreamville Festival, a daylong, multistage event hosted on the wide-open acreage of Dorothea Dix Park. Attendance surges to nearly 40,000 for the impressive jackpot of art, food, and musical talent (many acts are from Cole's own label). Previous performers include Big Sean, Nelly, and J. Cole himself. There is a mouthwatering array of food vendors, most local to North Carolina, and the live mural paintings and art installations transform Dix Park into a whimsical, artistic escape, or dare I say, Dreamville.

1030 Richardson Dr., info@dreamvillefest.com
dreamvillefest.com

TIP

Part of your ticket proceeds go to supporting the Dix Park Conservancy and the Dreamville Foundation. The Dix Park Conservancy is a nonprofit organization supporting the development and success of Dix Park, while the Dreamville Foundation provides support to young people and single-parent families in Fayetteville, North Carolina.

ENJOY THE ACME OF ARTS
AT DUKE ENERGY CENTER
FOR THE PERFORMING ARTS

Facing the Capitol building to the north, this elegant complex perches like a proud bookend on south Fayetteville Street, as if to announce, "Welcome to the pinnacle of Raleigh arts." Outside, Lichtin Plaza is an exclamation point to the magnificent, columned facade and a fitting stop to snap a few pics with the Raleigh skyline before showtime. Inside, the four concert halls, each with unique interiors and varying capacities, offer great diversity in grandiosity of experience, from the 2,400-capacity Memorial Auditorium to the 150-seat, black-box Kennedy Theatre. While playing host to popular touring acts like Broadway favorites and stand-up comedians, Duke Energy Center is also the permanent residence of Carolina Ballet, North Carolina Theatre, North Carolina Symphony, North Carolina Opera, and PineCone, Raleigh's traditional music and folk performing arts organization.

2 E South St., (919) 996-8700
dukeenergycenterraleigh.com

ENSNARE YOUR SENSES AT IMAX
AT MARBLES KIDS MUSEUM

In the cool darkness of the auditorium, a three-story screen springs to life and surround sound floods the airwaves. Not your typical day at the movies, the 3D IMAX experience, the only one in the state, is transcendent. The show schedule includes an enriching mix of the biggest blockbusters, as well as breathtaking nature documentaries. Working in conjunction with the educational programming at the museum, these are the crown jewels of the cinematic experience at the IMAX. The fourth wall falls, and you're swimming with dolphins, swinging through the jungle, journeying across outer space. It's nature in a new light, allowing you to examine the tiniest details and melt under the vastest vistas. Don't be alarmed when the lights come up and you're genuinely puzzled by your surroundings

201 E Hargett St., (919) 834-4040
marblesimax.org

EXPLORE A FULL SPECTRUM OF TALENT
AT HOPSCOTCH MUSIC FESTIVAL

Every September, an eclectic band of merry musicians descends on downtown Raleigh for a weekend-long musical bash. What makes it especially unique is that somewhere around a quarter of the acts are native North Carolinians. More than 120 bands and acts perform over the three-day stretch, covering every genre under the sun, from rock to hip-hop and folk to electronic. Mirroring the diversity of performances, music revelers of every kind flock to Hopscotch, solidifying it as a place to be for the green and mature, singles and couples, natives and weekenders. Whether you prefer smooth chords in a small dive bar or raucous rifts in a packed amphitheater, you'll find your tribe at Hopscotch.

info@hopscotchmusicfest.com
hopscotchmusicfest.com

TIP
Many of the clubs and venues within the Hopscotch domain host free daytime shindigs for anyone to enjoy. Party like it's your birthday, for free!

FIND YOUR FAVORITE FIDDLERS
AT IBMA BLUEGRASS LIVE!

Since 2013, the International Bluegrass Music Association (IBMA), a Nashville-based nonprofit and professional trade organization for the global bluegrass community, has teamed up with Raleigh organizers to host "the world's largest urban bluegrass festival and conference." A mix of professional conference, artist showcase, award ceremony, and music festival, "World of Bluegrass" is a banjo-bumpin', fiddle-flexin', five-day annual homecoming for the bluegrass community. For professionals and die-hards, the first three days are a must for networking, keynote addresses, official showcase acts, and a glittering awards ceremony. The final two days are reserved for the free music festival, IBMA Bluegrass Live! It spans various venues vast and small across downtown with heavyweight, Grammy-winning headliners like the Steep Canyon Rangers and the Travelin' McCourys.

(615) 256-3222
worldofbluegrass.org

NESTLE AMONG THE TREES
AT KOKA BOOTH AMPHITHEATRE

Outdoor concerts on the water? By all means! Koka Booth Amphitheatre is a resplendent structure on the edge of Symphony Lake. Sleek and impressive, it blends seamlessly with its natural surroundings. Excepting the wide-open spectator lawn, much of the campus is bursting with pines and hardwoods, giving it that nerve-calming, forest-bathing feel. Throughout summer, the venue hosts annual series, including the North Carolina Symphony Summerfest, Movies by Moonlight, and Pickin' in the Pines Bluegrass. Also on the calendar are fan-favorite touring acts like Chris Stapleton and Jack Johnson. During the holiday season, an absolutely imperative experience is the North Carolina Chinese Lantern Festival. It is a breathtaking, awe-inspiring display of colossal and intricately crafted LED lanterns depicting whimsical creatures, imaginative architecture, and everything in between.

8003 Regency Pkwy., Cary, (919) 462-2025
boothamphitheatre.com

BASK IN OUTDOOR ENTERTAINMENT OF EVERY KIND
AT JOSEPH M. BRYAN JR. THEATER

Vintage films and blockbusters, bluegrass and Americana, jazz and rock: it's all happening at the Joseph M. Bryan Jr. Theater. On the grounds of the North Carolina Museum of Art (NCMA), it's more park than playhouse, with an open-air amphitheater and surrounding fields to run and play. Every angle is abutted by panoramic views and larger-than-life artwork. Each summer, the NCMA hosts musical acts and entertainment in the amphitheater, where you can opt to get up close and personal with reserved seating or spread out with a picnic on the lawn. Occupying the horseshoe-shaped sandbox just beside the amphitheater are weekly outdoor movie screenings with nostalgic throwbacks and family-friendly favorites. Kick off your sneaks, bring your favorite picnic (and person), and soak up a starlit experience.

2110 Blue Ridge Rd., (919) 839-6262
ncartmuseum.org/mec-category/summer-concerts

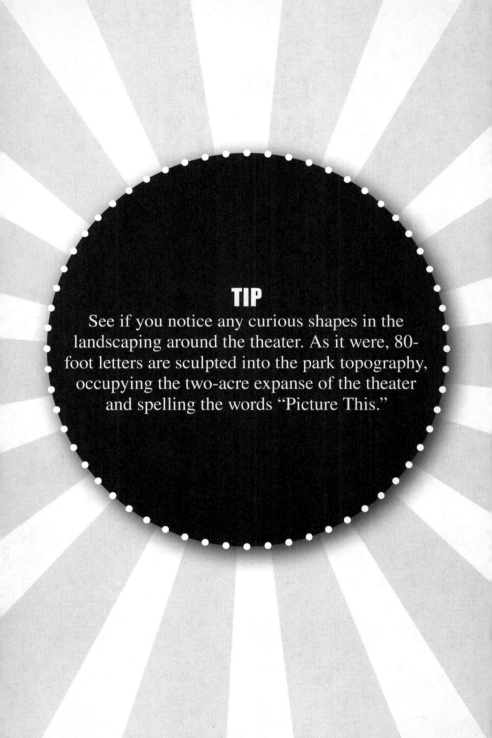

TIP

See if you notice any curious shapes in the landscaping around the theater. As it were, 80-foot letters are sculpted into the park topography, occupying the two-acre expanse of the theater and spelling the words "Picture This."

AMP UP YOUR HOLIDAY SPIRIT
AT MEADOW LIGHTS

What started as a simple, front yard manger scene has grown into a vast display of millions of lights where hordes of revelers are drawn in each season to experience the twinkling, North Pole-worthy wonderland. Driving in from the road, you're immediately immersed in dazzling scenes of castles and candy canes, flying pigs and dancing reindeer, Christmas trees and snowmen. It's free to enter and enjoy, but for just a couple of well-spent bucks more you can hop aboard the family-friendly train for a loop around the property. A trip down memory lane, the Old Country Store at the heart of Meadow Lights is packed with barrels of old-fashioned candy, coolers of vintage sodas, hot chocolate, apple cider, preserves, popcorn, and enough charm to last you 'til next Christmas.

4546 Godwin Lake Rd., Benson, (919) 669-5969
meadowlights.com

WATCH
SPORTS, SINGERS, AND
CIRCUS PERFORMERS
AT PNC ARENA

From Snoop Dogg to Céline Dion, PNC Arena hosts a staggering variety of entertainment. Conveniently located just west of the city, it is Raleigh's biggest (and quite possibly loudest during especially contentious sporting events) indoor stadium. It is home residence to the Carolina Hurricanes of the NHL and North Carolina State Wolfpack men's basketball. Famed family-oriented attractions have included the cheeky and wildly talented antics of the Harlem Globetrotters, the whimsical storytelling of Disney on Ice, and the colorful, logic-defying magic of the Ringling Brothers and Barnum & Bailey Circus. For the tailgate-keen, arrive early to sporting events for your own personal parking lot party. If concessions are more your speed, there are abundant options, both sweet and savory, once inside.

1400 Edwards Mill Rd., (919) 861-2300
pncarena.com

HAVE THE TIME OF YOUR LIFE
AT THE NORTH CAROLINA STATE FAIR

Every fall, the North Carolina Department of Agriculture hosts a dizzying bonanza of food and games, competition and crafts, animals, and agriculture. At the intersection of carnival and exposition, the North Carolina State Fair is equal parts exhilaration and nostalgia. First stop: Heritage Circle for live bluegrass and John Deere motor-churned ice cream. Next, on to the garden center for mind-bending horticultural creativity. Pick up a handmade craft in the Village of Yesteryear, then stop by the Graham Building for record-breaking pumpkins the size of small vehicles. When the sun goes down, hop on the State Fair SkyGazer for a stunning, bird's-eye view of the fairgrounds, all lit up. Rides and games are dispersed throughout, as are mouthwatering, seemingly limitless creations of fried everything.

4285 Trinity Rd., (919) 821-7400
ncstatefair.org

TIP

A real crowd pleaser is the Circle C Racing Pigs expo. Complete with little numbered bibs, the tiny, pink, four-legged contestants come flying out of their isolation booths and around the track, much to the delight of the onlookers. Check race times and show up early for an exciting trackside seat.

SUPPORT COMMUNITY ENTERTAINMENT
AT RALEIGH LITTLE THEATRE

In the throes of the Great Depression, a community theater blossomed in Raleigh. It was 1936, and ardent local artists teamed up with the Federal Theatre Project to build what has been a lasting commitment to affordable entertainment. The event schedule is thoughtfully curated, with a lineup including musicals, plays, concerts, family shows, Shakespeare, and film screenings. Arguably what makes the campus so timeless and unique is the 2,000-person-capacity outdoor Louise S. Stephenson Amphitheatre. Summer shows and screenings take place here, under the stars and swaddled by a lush and leafy arboretum. Just behind the amphitheater is the Rose Garden, a sensory wonderland of color and smell. It's a 60-bed plot with dozens of rose varieties, miniature and massive, from the palest yellow to the deepest red.

301 Pogue St., (919) 821-4579
raleighlittletheatre.org

SHIMMY UP BESIDE THE SKYLINE
AT RED HAT AMPHITHEATER

With room for approximately 6,000, Red Hat Amphitheater falls in the sweet spot of intimate and energetic. All summer long, touring acts land at the downtown venue, treating fans to an outdoor concert experience backed by invigorating views of the Raleigh skyline. Besides whoever is gracing the stage, another eye-popping display is the "Shimmer Wall," located to the right of the amphitheater when facing the stage. Formed from LED-backed metal plates and resembling a colossal oak tree (for Raleigh's nickname, "City of Oaks"), it is a public art installation spanning the entire western wall of the Raleigh Convention Center. Whimsy ensues when the wind blows, giving an illusion of rustling leaves. Come for your favorite act and revel in the cityscape magic.

500 S McDowell St., (919) 996-8500
redhatamphitheater.com

TIP
In addition to individual touring acts, don't miss Red Hat Amphitheater as a chief venue of the several music festivals taking place downtown.

THROW IT BACK
AT RIALTO THEATRE

The historic Rialto Theatre matches the throwback films it features. Originally opened in 1942, it's the longest-running, oldest movie theater in Raleigh. It's been spiffed up by renovation but has never forsaken the timeless vibes. Catch a flick Friday, Saturday, Sunday, or Monday at matinee and evening showings of foreign and independent films, documentaries, and old-school classics like *Vertigo*, *Breakfast at Tiffany's*, *The Godfather*, and *Pulp Fiction*. Or stay up for the midnight experience of *Rocky Horror Picture Show*, airing monthly on Fridays at midnight. With beer, wine, and champagne concessions, heavenly popcorn aromas, and a free screening of the Oscars every year, the Rialto is a cherished cornerstone of vintage Raleigh and a nostalgic escape for casual viewers and cinephiles alike.

1620 Glenwood Ave., (919) 856-0111
ambassadorcinemas.com

TIP
Make it a double feature and stop by Hayes Barton Café, located just down the street in the Five Points neighborhood, for a pre- or post-picture slice of cake.

GUFFAW AND REFLECT
AT THEATRE IN THE PARK

A hidden gem with national clout and devoted patrons, Theatre in the Park brings big-time talent to small-town charm. Mastermind of the playhouse and multi-hyphenate creative, longtime executive director Ira David Wood III is a Raleigh visionary, recognized internationally with a glittering awards résumé. Theatre in the Park, so named for its perch inside Pullen Park, is an intimate indoor theater heralded for exquisite presentations of diverse material. The piéce de résistance is the annual production of *A Christmas Carol*. Wood himself leads the cast as curmudgeonly Scrooge in a musically outfitted, gut-bustlingly hilarious, ingenious adaptation of the Dickens classic. Since its debut in 1974, it has been adoringly regarded as an annual highlight in Raleigh, easily selling out the Memorial Auditorium year after year.

107 Pullen Rd., (919) 831-6058
theatreinthepark.com

SPORTS
AND RECREATION

FROLIC WITH FAIRIES
AT ANNIE LOUISE WILKERSON, MD, NATURE PRESERVE PARK

As the first designated nature preserve in Raleigh, its essence is rooted in wildlife. Dr. Wilkerson, a celebrated Raleigh obstetrician, deeded her land to the City of Raleigh, asking that it be used chiefly for nature education. The big, open fields bring a blustery, *Sound of Music* enthusiasm to the landscape, while wooded trails are secluded, serene, and dusted with fairy magic (look for their little houses in the Fairyland Forest!). Stop in Dr. Wilkerson's former home, now the Education Center, for a free loaner backpack provisioned with quintessential adventure equipment. The preserve also includes a connector segment to the Mountains-to-Sea Trail. Head east (a right turn if coming from the connector) and hike several miles to Falls Lake Dam for panoramic views of the water.

5229 Awls Haven Dr., (919) 996-6764
raleighnc.gov/places/annie-louise-wilkerson-md-nature-preserve

HIKE, PLAY, PICNIC, AND KAYAK
AT BLUE JAY POINT COUNTY PARK

Blue Jay is cozied up on the southern shores of Falls Lake and makes a compelling argument to spend the entire day outside. The miles-long wooded trail system by the water's edge is just adventurous enough to be a solid hike or run without excluding the possibility of an easygoing amble. Included in the trails are several access points to picnic by the water or launch a kayak and get a seaward view of the peninsula and adjacent mini-island. Full-time staff at Blue Jay host regular events and excursions around the park for students to connect with the surrounding ecosystem. Blue Jay also is home to acres of open fields and playgrounds. Get some mulch in your shoes for good measure, and really unleash your inner youngster.

3200 Pleasant Union Church Rd., (919) 870-4330
wakegov.com/departments-government/parks-recreation-and-open-space/
all-parks-trails/blue-jay-point-county-park

KEEP UP WITH NHL ACTION
WITH THE CAROLINA HURRICANES

It's quite a spectacle: players zip after rogue pucks and smash into the sideboards with enough force to rattle your teeth, all the while performing complex footwork on ice skates. As longtime Hurricanes play-by-play announcer John Forslund would say, "That's hockey, baby!" Stanley Cup champions in 2006, the "Canes" are a beloved staple of the sports scene in Raleigh. Members of the NHL, they play rousing home games at the massive PNC Arena. Look out for team mascot Stormy the Ice Hog skating around, hyping the crowd, and whipping out Canes T-shirts. In recent years, the Hurricanes have taken to ending their games with an elaborately choreographed "Storm Surge" formation to entertain, honor, and celebrate victory with the fans.

1400 Edwards Mill Rd., (919) 861-2300
nhl.com/hurricanes

TIP
For a more refined, group-friendly experience, look for box seat opportunities. When the team is on the road, head to the Carolina Ale House for the official, fan-centric Canes watch party.

SHOOT FOR PAR OR TOSS FOR FUN
AT DIAVOLO AT NEW HOPE DISC GOLF

It sounds simple enough: grab a disc, tee off, and throw until you land it in the basket. But with the smallest gaps between trees, water shots, and formidable yardage to cover, this disc golf course presents quite a stimulating challenge. Disc golf has the wonderful bandwidth to entertain focused competitors and leisurely dabblers alike. The 22-hole course fuses with its natural surroundings, winding through woods and open fields, supplying varied shot lengths and multiple tee boxes for players of differing levels. Bring your own discs (. . . and drinks) and strike up a little friendly competition, or if you tire of tossing, enjoy a serene walk with your fellow frolfers. Of note, Diavolo was ranked in the top 10 on UDisc's list of the world's best disc golf courses for 2021.

2584 New Hope Church Rd., Cary, (919) 380-2781
townofcary.org/recreation-enjoyment/parks-greenways-environment/parks/
middle-creek-school-park/diavolo-new-hope-disc-golf-course

FEAST YOUR EYES ON SUNFLOWER CITY
AT DOROTHEA DIX PARK

Open seven days a week and just half a mile from downtown, Dix Park is Raleigh's biggest public park. Ancient, noble oaks and wide-open spaces abound, framed by the stoic Raleigh skyline. The Big Field is perfect for pickup games and picnics, even drone-spotting, as it's one of the few unmanned-aerial-aircraft-approved spots in the area. Check the park schedule for free, outdoor group classes like yoga and tai chi. It also has a designated dogs-off-lead area, where your four-legged friend can socialize and roam free. Perhaps the biggest draw of Dix Park, however, is Flowers Field. Every summer, thousands of sunflowers bloom across the acreage in a postcard picture of golden beauty, a must-see Raleigh landscape.

2105 Umstead Dr., (919) 996-3255
dixpark.org

TIP

Available parking during work hours may be limited, as many spots are permitted to North Carolina Department of Health and Human Services employees. Consider walking or biking in using the Rocky Branch portion of the Capital Area Greenway Trail.

ENTHUSE IN THE OUTDOORS
AT FALLS LAKE STATE RECREATION AREA

Falls Lake is Raleigh's 12,000-acre, pristine reservoir and the acme of Raleigh outdoor recreation. Its undeveloped, forested shores are popular for hiking, biking, picnicking, and camping, while the lake proper is prime real estate for boating, swimming, paddling, and fishing. Reserve your spot at one of 300 campsites or take to the dog-friendly, wooded trails extending approximately 60 miles along the water's edge, from the northwest corner all the way to the southeastern dam at the mouth of the Neuse River. The trail system, part of the state Mountains-to-Sea Trail, is an epic adventure through surprisingly diverse topography and can easily be broken into smaller sections for a day hike. With the abundance of trails, beaches, access points, campgrounds, and unblemished views, it's worth exploring every corner.

Park Office and Information Center
13304 Creedmoor Rd., Wake Forest, (919) 676-1027
ncparks.gov/visit/parks/fala/main.php

SWING THROUGH THE CANOPY
AT GO APE ZIPLINE
AND ADVENTURE PARK

A change in perspective can be refreshing. In this case, literally so. Ever craved a skyward approach to a walk in the woods? This is the quest for you. Go Ape makes its home at Blue Jay Point County Park, and while hikers take to the trails below, the Tarzan-channeling brave-of-heart can explore an entirely different sector of the forest. Step into a harness, attach your tether to the cables running above each challenge, and leap! Test your resolve across hanging obstacles, ziplines, and free-fall swings. A safe yet nevertheless heart-thumping experience, adults and kids alike will delight in dappled views, wind-in-the-hair thrills, and a unique adventure usually reserved for our primate cousins.

3200 Pleasant Union Church Rd., (800) 971-8271
goape.com/location/north-carolina-raleigh-durham

DISCOVER PANORAMIC VISTAS OF RALEIGH
AT GREEN HILLS COUNTY PARK

The first thing you'll notice when driving into the park is the colossal, grassy mound at its center. The formidable centerpiece marks the county landfill that occupied the space before it was converted into a park, circa 2008. Winding up the side is a gravel trail leading to the Big Hill pinnacle and some of the most unparalleled views of Raleigh. Don't forget your picnic! Back on the main grounds, an expansive, mulched playground, complete with a topsy-turvy rock wall, is sure to win the hearts of youngsters, while off-road hikers and bikers will enjoy the two miles of multi-use trail. For the fearless cyclists, test your prowess on the mountain bike skills course.

9300 Deponie Dr., (919) 870-4330
wakegov.com/departments-government/parks-recreation-and-open-space/
all-parks-trails/green-hills-county-park

TIP

Green Hills continues to serve as an important multi-use recycling center and source of green energy. As organic materials decompose within the covered landfill, methane gases are collected and siphoned to nearby industries for fuel. Drop off your food scraps at the recycling center for composting, courtesy of Wake County.

HIKE AMONG HISTORY
AT HISTORIC YATES MILL COUNTY PARK

The last of its kind in Wake County, this fully operational, 18th-century gristmill served a crucial role in the community for over 200 years. Rustic and impressive, it roosts on the edge of Yates Mill Pond dam, where water rushes over, powering the grain-grinding operation within. Learning and recreational opportunities abound around the park, including historical exhibits within the A. E. Finley Center for Education and Research and guided tours of the mill, complete with corn-grinding and historically outfitted demonstrators once a month. The easygoing Millpond Trail curves right around the pond; the more arduous High Ridge Trail winds through forests along the bluffs; and the out-and-back Creekside Trail takes you through the Steep Hill Creek wetlands via footbridges and boardwalks.

4620 Lake Wheeler Rd., (919) 856-6675
wakegov.com/parks/yatesmill/Pages/default.aspx

TIP
Stop by Howling Cow Creamery, the North Carolina State University operation a hop and a skip up the road, for post-hike frozen goodness.

APPRECIATE FLORAL THEMES
AT J. C. RAULSTON ARBORETUM

Free, colorful, diverse, brimming with life: what's not to love? This arboretum, owned and operated by North Carolina State University, is just a couple of miles west of the main campus; it is open to the public and dedicated to the science and aesthetics of horticulture. Make a start on the McSwain Education Center rooftop terrace for a bird's-eye peep at the 10 acres below. Back on the ground, wind through dedicated beds housing plants of similar origin, with themes like winter and Japanese gardens, and flora with drought resistance or underground storage organs. The White Garden is a picture of elegance and a popular venue for foliage-friendly weddings. Look for the garden's charming "Air Bee and Bee," an elaborately built wooden hotel for the arboretum's pollinators.

4415 Beryl Rd., (919) 515-3132
jcra.ncsu.edu

TIP
Though there are plenty of benches and resting spots, many of the paths are stone and pebble and may not be accessible for everyone.

TRAIPSE THROUGH RARE FLORA
AT JUNIPER LEVEL BOTANIC GARDEN

In 1988, Juniper Level was an abandoned, acidic tobacco field south of Raleigh. With meticulous cultivation, the soil has been rebalanced, land repurposed, and momentum restored. Now home to over 25,000 different taxa of plants, it's a vivacious intersection of botany and horticulture, the owners arguably having achieved their mission to become the "most unique botanic garden in the world." What makes Juniper Level so rare is literally sprouting from the ground. You'll find worldly specimens flourishing here in a heroic effort to conserve what has become extinct in the wild. Wind your way through the gardens, beside trickling waterfalls, and under leafy canopies. Helpfully, plants are labeled throughout, so if one strikes your fancy, you can take home seeds from the nursery and re-create your own meditative oasis.

9241 Sauls Rd., (919) 772-4794
jlbg.org

TIP

The garden offers free admission but is open to the
public only two weekends each season. Check the
"open house" dates when planning your visit.

PADDLE AND PLAY
AT LAKE JOHNSON PARK

Bursting with natural beauty, Lake Johnson delivers every time in the outdoor fun department. Rent a kayak or paddleboard from the Waterfront Center and take in the wooded shoreline and serene waters. Ideal for rollers and strollers, the three-mile, paved Greenway Trail winds around the east side of the lake and connects to the expansive, citywide Capital Area Greenway system. The westerly walk around Lake Johnson is a lesser-trafficked, natural-surface trail for the keen hiker. Hit the public pool and splash pad for a post-hike cooldown. Visitors can also take advantage of abundant group programming. Classes for all ages run the gamut from birding, fishing, sailing, and night paddling all the way to yoga and ballroom dancing.

4601 Avent Ferry Rd., (919) 996-3141
raleighnc.gov/places/lake-johnson-park

RUN, WOLF DOWN A DOZEN DOUGHNUTS, RUN BACK

AT THE KRISPY KREME CHALLENGE

This isn't your average road race. It started as a dare among friends in 2004 and has since become an absurdly challenging, wildly spirited, coveted annual event, raising millions of dollars to benefit North Carolina Children's Hospital. It begins and ends at the Memorial Belltower on North Carolina State University's campus. Participants run 2.5 miles to Krispy Kreme, attempt to down one dozen glazed doughnuts, then run back in hopefully under an hour. Considered a bucket list item for undergraduates, the event requires heroic levels of athleticism and steely determination, not to mention iron digestive resilience. Despite hordes of fierce competitors, there are also plenty of participants who opt to walk or jog without the mid-race, sugar-fueled eat-a-thon, while others are there for exactly that.

2011 Hillsborough St.
krispykremechallenge.com

TEE IT UP ON AN ARNOLD PALMER ORIGINAL
AT LONNIE POOLE GOLF COURSE

Perhaps the most well-regarded public course in the area, Lonnie Poole was designed by golf king Arnold Palmer himself and is home to the North Carolina State University golf team. The par-72 course presents a stout and intriguing challenge to even the most experienced, and it has played host to many important tournaments and qualifiers, both collegiate and professional. With beautifully varied terrain, rolling hills, and tall, wispy fescue, it brims with a natural character reminiscent of the Scottish Highlands. It is rewarding of the well-executed shot and punishing of the wayward, yet impeccable maintenance—tee to green—ensures a fair matchup. The majestic landscape and ever-charming Raleigh skyline backdrop (particularly the iconic view on the 11th tee box) provide as majestic a vista as any around.

1509 Main Campus Dr., (919) 515-6527
lonniepoolegolfcourse.com

TIP
Hit up the state-of-the-art practice facility for range time, putting, bunker play, and club fitting.

SPEND THE DAY
AT THE WORLD'S LARGEST NATURAL-HABITAT ZOO AT NORTH CAROLINA ZOO

While there is much bustle within the city limits, this menagerie of magnificent wildlife is well worth a little extra trekking. About an hour and a half west of Raleigh, the North Carolina Zoo happens to be the largest natural-habitat zoological park in the world. It's split into two sections, North America and Africa, both reflective of the incredible diversity across each continent. Strategize your visit around feeding times, as these offer some of the most vibrant experiences and the chance to ask questions of the zookeepers. Roll out with Zoofari for an open-air, vehicular tour through the Grasslands, or stop at the Acacia Station treetop deck and hold out a scrap of lettuce for the giraffes to slurp up with their long, purple tongues.

4401 Zoo Pkwy., Asheboro, (336) 879-7000
nczoo.org

TIP
Refreshments for humans are plentiful as well, with several locally sourced restaurants and concession stands throughout.

ROLL THROUGH WOODS AND WETLANDS
ON THE NEUSE RIVER GREENWAY TRAIL

Part of the 100-mile Capital Area Greenway system, the Neuse River trail takes up residence right along the water and offers some of the most picturesque scenery of the whole greenway. There are several spots to make a start along the trail, but for the unabridged experience (including, as it were, quite a few bridges), begin at the Falls Lake trailhead, adjacent to the dam. From here to the Johnston County line is 27.5 miles of uninterrupted, paved, flat passage through forests, historic sites, nature preserves, and marshes. It's an out-and-back path, so you have the option to park a car at either end or brave the double distance. Bikers, runners, walkers, skippers, rollerbladers, forest bathers, and any other creative movers are welcome!

Falls Lake Tailrace Parking
12101 Old Falls of Neuse Rd., Wake Forest, (919) 846-9332
raleighnc.gov/places/neuse-river-greenway-trail

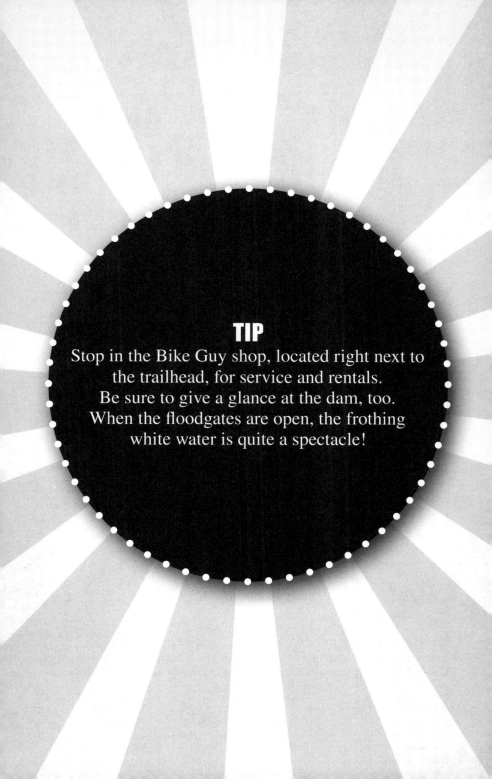

TIP

Stop in the Bike Guy shop, located right next to
the trailhead, for service and rentals.
Be sure to give a glance at the dam, too.
When the floodgates are open, the frothing
white water is quite a spectacle!

FROLIC, FEAST, AND HEAT UP YOUR FALL
AT PHILLIPS FARMS

This bucolic haven has it all, but let's start with food, obviously. Phillips Farms hosts a weekend market in the spring and summer, with food trucks and local vendors selling a cornucopia of rainbow produce. Most weekends are themed to celebrate the abundance of the season, with day festivals like berry, peach, watermelon, bbq, and ice cream. In September, Phillips transforms into an autumn adventure, with an epically expansive corn maze, wagon ride, pick-your-own pumpkin patch, haunted farm, and family fun park brimming with carnival-level creativity. The pumpkin catapult, gigantic bounce pillows, pygmy goats, human foosball, pedal cart races, and massive tube swing just barely scratch the surface of this deep dive into good-for-the-soul, sun-soaked, fresh-air fun on the farm.

6701 Good Hope Church Rd., Cary, (919) 377-8989
phillipsfarmsofcary.com

TIP
Follow along on the Facebook page for fast updates about produce, vendors, festivals, and inclement weather announcements.

GET YOUR FOOTBALL FIX
AT WakeMed SOCCER PARK

Home to not one but two professional teams, this sports complex is a soccer mecca. After returning to North Carolina from New York in 2017, the North Carolina Courage of the National Women's Soccer League has racked up some impressive stats in just a few short years (2018 and 2019 regular season and playoff champs). The North Carolina Football Club (NCFC), current member of United Soccer League One, also plays its home matches at the 10,000-capacity main arena, Sahlen's Stadium. For an immersive evening, enjoy a pre-game rendezvous at one of several participating game-day restaurants (be sure to check the NCFC website for updates). From there, the Red & Blue Express shuttles fans to the game for free. No need for stressful parking sagas or designated drivers here!

101 Soccer Park Dr., Cary, (919) 858-0464
northcarolinafc.com

GAMBOL ABOUT
ONE OF THE WORLD'S OLDEST
AMUSEMENT PARKS AT PULLEN PARK

Around since 1887 and the first public park in North Carolina, Pullen Park has enjoyed meticulous maintenance over the years and marries old-world allure with modern renovations. The greenery-shrouded pathways lead to an expansive playground, open fields for softball or carefree roaming, lighted tennis courts, and the community aquatic and activity centers. Catch a ride on the miniature train for a full tour of the grounds, or rent a pedal boat for a waterside excursion on Lake Howell. Above all, don't miss the antique Dentzel carousel. Built in 1911, it has been beautifully restored and designated as a Raleigh Historic Landmark. Take a lap around the whimsical, mirrored track on the back of a giraffe and settle into a world of genteel charm.

520 Ashe Ave., (919) 996-6468
raleighnc.gov/places/pullen-park

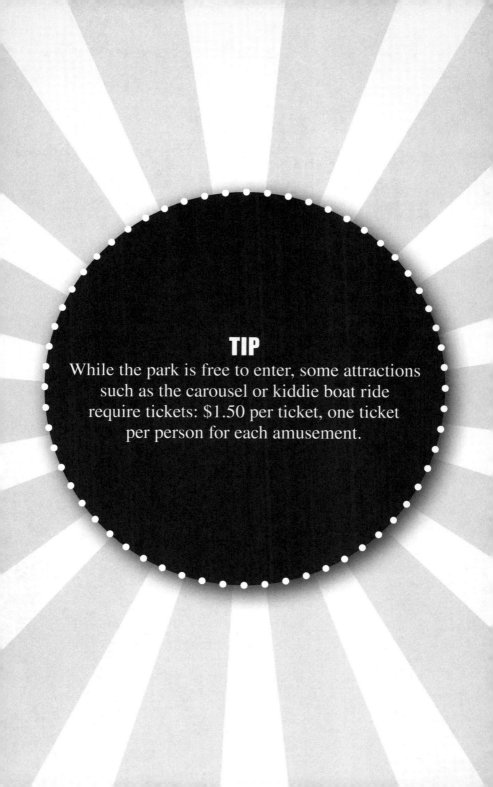

TIP

While the park is free to enter, some attractions
such as the carousel or kiddie boat ride
require tickets: $1.50 per ticket, one ticket
per person for each amusement.

PADDLE THROUGH CYPRESS
AT ROBERTSON MILLPOND PRESERVE

A rare blackwater swamp to the east of Raleigh, this teeming, cypress oasis is one of a kind in the county and coveted for its natural serenity and history. While the gristmill, built circa 1820, has been dismantled due to disrepair, the dam formed from masonry and earth still stands across Buffalo Creek, allowing for unparalleled paddling through the swamp. Bring your own (non-motorized) vessel and cast off into the pond via the shoreline or Americans with Disabilities Act (ADA)-accessible launch. A buoy-marked circuit takes you clockwise through the waters on a 1.15-mile, circular tour of the swamp. In this pristine setting, allow nature to do the talking as you glide through the tannin-stained habitat of resident birds and beavers, reptiles, and fish.

6333 Robertson Pond Rd., Wendell, (919) 604-9326
wakegov.com/parks/robertsonmillpond

SHARPEN YOUR CLIMBING PROWESS
AT TRIANGLE ROCK CLUB

No longer just for the van-living, adrenaline-fueled junkies of Yosemite Valley, climbing has surged in popularity among casual and dedicated athletes alike, thanks to its plethora of wellness benefits and endorphin-inducing thrills. Triangle Rock Club (TRC) especially has been celebrated for its inclusive offerings for beginning dabblers, longtime die-hards, and individuals with disabilities seeking an adaptive climbing approach. Both Raleigh-area TRC indoor gyms feature fitness space and group classes alongside bouldering and rope climbing. Morrisville, with its 55-foot walls and extensive, bolted sport climbing section, is ideal for endurance, while the cavernous bouldering area of North Raleigh is a favorite for power and strength training. Test it out temporarily with a day pass, or join the gym for unlimited access to all TRC facilities.

Morrisville (West Raleigh)
102 Pheasant Wood Ct., Morrisville, (919) 463-7625
trianglerockclub.com/morrisville

North Raleigh
6022 Duraleigh Rd., (919) 803-5534
trianglerockclub.com/raleigh

DITCH THE MOTOR
AT WILLIAM B. UMSTEAD STATE PARK

Whether you are a runner, hiker, cyclist, equestrian, nature-reveler, or a delightful combination of the above, this is your haven for all things nature. Umstead is chock-full of wooded foot trails, packed gravel lanes, picnic spots, and enough flora to turn your skin green, all on protected land with absolutely no motorized transport passing through. The park sprawls between Interstate 40 and US Route 70 with two main entrances along each highway, though there are a handful of other convenient access points with parking. Try the Sycamore Trail for a streamside hike or jaunt. The Cedar Ridge multi-use trail is a winding roller coaster of a ride, and a must-do for the adventurous biker. Don't miss the creek crossing at the end!

US Route 70
8801 Glenwood Ave.

Interstate 40
2100 N Harrison Ave., Cary

(919) 571-4170
ncparks.gov/william-b-umstead-state-park

TIP

Look out for a massive, intricate display of chainsaw art, carved into a fallen tree just off to the side of the Graylyn multi-use trail. If biking, opt for bigger, hybrid tires, as there are no paved lanes within the park.

CULTURE
AND HISTORY

REIMAGINE PAINTINGS AS FLORAL ARRANGEMENTS
AT ART IN BLOOM

Every year, the West Building of the North Carolina Museum of Art is adorned with thousands of vivacious blooms in eye-popping floral interpretations of the permanent collection. This two-weekend event is an annual staple for anyone appreciative of evocative aesthetics. Area designers, florists, and hobbyists are invited to participate, each randomly assigned to emulate a particular museum work using flowers and greenery. Some towering, others scaled down, the installations are a reinterpretation of the original medium. Artists assemble their creations on-site, having painstakingly prepared embellishments in advance, over the course of hundreds of hours in some cases. They're the most photogenic flowers you've ever seen, perfectly paired with live music, floral-themed refreshments from the café, and enlightening demonstrations, lectures, and workshops.

2110 Blue Ridge Rd., (919) 839-6262
ncartmuseum.org

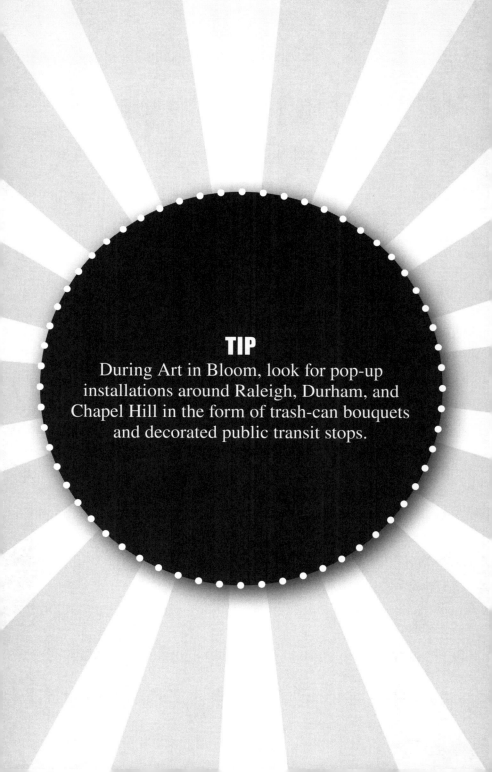

TIP

During Art in Bloom, look for pop-up installations around Raleigh, Durham, and Chapel Hill in the form of trash-can bouquets and decorated public transit stops.

SHOP HANDMADE AND SPECTATE
AT ARTSPLOSURE:
THE RALEIGH ARTS FESTIVAL

Running since 1980, this is Raleigh's most tenured arts festival, completely free and so abundant with expression there's something for everyone to appreciate. Over 150 regional and national visual artists descend on downtown Raleigh with their tents and tables like a colorful wave. This two-day market features paintings, jewelry, ceramics, sculptures, photography, and more. With food and beverage trucks, live music, and art installations on display throughout the area, it's as much stimulating entertainment as it is the perfect place to round out your collection with something handmade and unique. There are crafts for kids and accommodations for visitors with accessibility needs. It's a rare opportunity to directly communicate with and support artists who may just be the masterminds behind your new favorite painting or mug.

Fayetteville St., (919) 832-8699
artsplosure.org

SWITCH IT UP
AT CONTEMPORARY
ART MUSEUM RALEIGH

The Contemporary Art Museum (CAM), the actual building itself, is a work of art. A sweeping, angular awning, embellished with geometric circles, smartens the exterior of this former produce building in Raleigh's Warehouse District. It's clean and quirky, reminiscent of the space inside. A non-collecting organization, CAM displays thought-provoking, modern work by living artists throughout the 20,000-square-foot space, with an ever-changing inventory of creativity. Many of the displays employ innovative techniques like videography and sound, giving the museum an impressive range of media. Admission is free; the art and fashion are a combination of edgy, gritty, warm, and chic (plus lots more); and the space is filled with soothing natural light. It's pretty much the perfect recipe for an imaginative experience.

409 W Martin St., (919) 261-5920
camraleigh.org

CHERISH HOMETOWN HISTORY
AT THE CITY OF RALEIGH MUSEUM

In the heart of downtown, on Fayetteville Street, the historic Briggs Hardware Building has been repurposed to celebrate Raleigh's legendary pioneers and leaders, city government, land usage and development, the fight for civil rights, and past and present stories of the city's life and character. A fitting place for the City of Raleigh (COR) Museum, this four-story, late-19th-century Victorian Gothic building is designated as "Raleigh's first skyscraper" and has housed many notable local organizations, such as Raleigh Little Theatre, the YMCA, the Oak City Guard, and now the COR Museum. Occupying the bottom two levels, the museum is intimate and approachable, like Raleigh herself, with exhibits reflecting milestones that have solidified the city as both a heartwarming hometown and entrepreneurial epicenter. Admission is free and natural lighting is abundant, thanks to the rooftop skylight.

220 Fayetteville St., (919) 996-2220
cityofraleighmuseum.org

REFLECT ON CIVIL RIGHTS STRIDES
AT THE DR. MARTIN LUTHER KING JR. MEMORIAL GARDENS

At the corner of Martin Luther King Jr. Boulevard and Rock Quarry Road, a life-size likeness of Dr. King stands nobly over the bustling intersection. A small but important landmark along the Civil Rights Trail, Dr. Martin Luther King Jr. Memorial Gardens is the first of its kind in the United States: a public park dedicated to the civil rights movement and its heroic leader. In addition to the bronze statue of Dr. King, a granite water monument pays homage to other area civil rights pioneers, with etchings of their names and Dr. King's words, "Until justice rolls down like water and righteousness like a mighty stream." Surrounded by floral landscaping, the monument and nearby picnic shelter are perfect spots for an outdoor meal while reflecting on Dr. King's irreplaceable legacy.

1215 Martin Luther King Jr. Blvd., (919) 996-4115
raleighnc.gov/parks/content/parksrec/articles/parks/mlkgardens.html

STROLL AMONG RALEIGH'S LEGENDS AND PIONEERS
AT HISTORIC OAKWOOD CEMETERY

Formerly part of the Mordecai estate, the cemetery land was donated by Henry Mordecai to be used as a resting place for the South's fallen soldiers. In contrast to traditional grid plots adjacent to a church, this cemetery, founded in 1869, is as much beautiful park as it is sacred burial ground. Shady oaks and dogwoods cradle the landscape, a serene natural backdrop to the elaborate and artistic mausoleums and headstones. Fall is a particularly picturesque time to wander the brick pathways, framed by vividly colorful leaves. Each October, Burning Coal Theatre presents short, outdoor plays based on the lives of cemetery residents and their contemporaries. Whenever you visit, a leisurely, meandering stroll across this historic landscape will reveal the resting places of some of Raleigh's bravest and brightest leaders.

701 Oakwood Ave., (919) 832-6077
historicoakwoodcemetery.org

DESIGN
YOUR UNIQUE EVENING
AT FIRST FRIDAY RALEIGH

For free spirits and independent adventurers, First Friday is a vibrant way to enjoy Raleigh's downtown art scene. Mirroring the name, this event takes place on the first Friday of every month from 6 to 9 p.m., when participating galleries, retailers, and restaurants feature special exhibits, discounts, deals, live music, and other perks. Downtown Raleigh Alliance presents these pop-up evenings and has a designated website to plan your trip. There, you can select the participating events that interest you, and pin drops of your itinerary will display on a digital map. Enjoy scrumptious desserts, cocktails, and refreshments; snap photos of Raleigh's new and storied murals; wander through galleries; and personally meet the artists behind the work. Support your local entrepreneurs and feel their gratitude in return.

(919) 832-1231
downtownraleigh.org/first-friday-raleigh/events

GET LOST IN ANOTHER UNIVERSE
AT GalaxyCon RALEIGH

GalaxyCon is a magical jackpot of superheroes, sci-fi, gaming, anime, comics, pop culture, and many thousands of die-hard cosplayers. If you're a fan of any of the above, this four-day festival is an unmatched, essential experience. Upwards of 50,000 enthusiasts descend on the Raleigh Convention Center, many costumed to portray their favorite fictional characters. The opportunity for engagement is boundless, with cosplay contests, dance parties, gaming tournaments, and celebrity experiences. Attend Q&A panels, photo ops, and autograph signings with your favorite screen and voice actors, wrestlers, comic creators, and other talented entertainers. With a stacked lineup of performers and some of the most elaborate costumes conceived by humankind, this fervent celebration of creativity is hands-down the most intriguing event at which to people/ character watch.

Raleigh Convention Center
500 S Salisbury St., (919) 907-0424
galaxycon.com/raleigh

COMMEMORATE LOCAL AND INTERNATIONAL ARTISTS
AT THE GREGG MUSEUM OF ART AND DESIGN

Located on North Carolina State University's North Campus, this free museum affords a unique opportunity to enjoy global artwork in the context of homegrown culture. The museum occupies the original brick North Carolina State Chancellor's Residence, along with a sleek, new extension, making the combined facade an apropos mixture of rustic and chic. Collections—both rotating and permanent—feature local and global paintings, textiles, ceramics, artifacts, furniture, and photography, as well as the largest collection of creations anywhere made by self-taught North Carolina artists. The surrounding grounds are studded with multi-tiered landscaping, brick walkways, rippling lawns, and plenty of inviting space for picnicking, playing, and reflecting. A true community gem, the museum is within walking distance of numerous restaurants and cafés, the North Carolina State Belltower, and Pullen Park.

1903 Hillsborough St., (919) 515-3503
gregg.arts.ncsu.edu

CRUISE AROUND TOWN ON STORIED WHEELS
WITH HISTORIC RALEIGH TROLLEY

On weekends from March through December, hop aboard Raleigh's most charming transportation: the Raleigh Trolley! Modeled after the original city trolleys from the early 1900s (but with updated machinery), these adorable, red trams take to the streets of downtown for hour-long tours. On Saturday, the trolley conveniently departs from Mordecai Historic Park, making it the perfect endcap to a tour of the surrounding village grounds. On Sunday, it rolls out of Moore Square. The tour guide will wheel you around some of Raleigh's most iconic landmarks, such as the Joel Lane Museum House, City Market, and Bicentennial Plaza. Another fun perk: you can rent a trolley for group transportation and dazzle your wedding, event, or party guests with a blast from the past on wheels.

1 Mimosa St., (919) 996-4364
raleighnc.gov/supportpages/historic-raleigh-trolley

UNLEASH YOUR IMAGINATION
AT THE MARBLES KIDS MUSEUM

All you have to do is show up, and Marbles will meet you with unequivocal entertainment. One of the most highly recommended activities for families in Raleigh, the museum is something of a fusion of Willy Wonka's factory, Thomas Edison's lab, and Dr. Seuss's clever universe. It's a kid's take on a grownup world, with eye-popping, attention-grabbing displays designed for discovery, play, problem-solving, and most of all, interaction. In each exhibit, there are things to pick up, build, roll around, jump on, slide through, color with, splash, squeeze, and create. In this colorful world, kids (and their grown people) can compose music, build giant LEGO castles, hula hoop, race cars, explore agriculture, generate energy . . . the list, like a robust imagination, is bottomless and bright.

201 E Hargett St., (919) 834-4040
marbleskidsmuseum.org

VISIT THE BIRTH HOME OF A US PRESIDENT
AT MORDECAI HISTORIC PARK

In 1785, Joel Lane, a notable contributor to the founding of Wake County, built a modest home for his son and daughter-in-law at the center of the family plantation. A later expansion transformed the little dwelling into the Greek Revival mansion that stands today. Nostalgic and intriguing, the Mordecai (pronounced *more*-duh-key) House is the oldest in Raleigh still in its original location. The house and its surrounding buildings offer an intimate brush with history, as 80 percent of the furnishings are original. In 1968, the 3.2-acre property was reimagined into a small, colonial village with the addition of St. Mark's Chapel, Allen Kitchen, Badger-Iredell Law Office, and President Andrew Johnson's tiny birthplace home, all well-preserved and open to visitors.

1 Mimosa St., (919) 996-4364
raleighnc.gov/places/mordecai-historic-park

TIP
Guided tours of the Mordecai House, grounds, and village buildings are offered hourly, but are not available when school groups are on-site.

LEARN ABOUT CONTRIBUTIONS FROM OUR STATE
AT THE NORTH CAROLINA MUSEUM OF HISTORY

North Carolina is a state of many monumental beginnings, from the Wright brothers' pioneering flight to the first state university. In the Museum of History, these groundbreaking milestones plus many more are well-documented alongside the heroes and renegades who have contributed to North Carolina's vibrancy. Every exhibit is curated to capture your attention, with interactive elements and re-created historical conditions. There are permanent exhibits, such as "The Story of North Carolina," with artifacts dating back many thousands of years. Another favorite is the North Carolina Sports Hall of Fame, where you can view jerseys, equipment, and memorabilia of some of our state's most preeminent athletes (Michael Jordan? Naturally). In the temporary exhibits, learn about broader world events and eras and how North Carolina has contributed. The state song and toast says it best: Here's to "Down Home," the Old North State!

5 E Edenton St., (919) 814-7000
ncmuseumofhistory.org

EXPLORE AN EXPANSIVE ARTISTIC CAMPUS
AT THE NORTH CAROLINA MUSEUM OF ART

The North Carolina Museum of Art (NCMA) is everything good and inspiring about civic investment: access to world-renowned artwork, inviting green space, and community-driven support of public exhibitions. A robust permanent collection features pieces from North America, Europe, and Africa, among many other regions and periods. Outside, the 164-acre Museum Park is a majestic landscape of open fields, trails (connected to the Capital Area Greenway), and sculptures like *Gyre*, a grouping of three orange-hued, earthen rings situated on the grounds like gigantic portals to a whimsical beyond. Among the outdoor installations, don't miss *Cloud Chamber for the Trees and Sky*. Using optics similar to those of a camera, this little round hut (akin to a hobbit house) projects a mirror image of the outside forest onto the interior of the chamber.

2110 Blue Ridge Rd., (919) 839-6262
ncartmuseum.org

TIP
Batch a meal into your museum experience with offerings from the two resident cafés. Order picnic baskets in advance for weekend outdoor dining in the Museum Park and for events at the Joseph M. Bryan Jr. Theater.

ABSORB A VAST VARIETY OF WONDERS
AT THE NORTH CAROLINA MUSEUM OF NATURAL SCIENCES

Among the free and enriching activities around Raleigh, this one is a showstopper. Journey through North Carolina and around the globe, under the ocean, inside living bodies, across eons, beyond the atmosphere, and inward to the smallest cells and particles. Keep your head on a swivel, because there is something awe-inspiring in every corner. Hands-on experiences (seriously, you're encouraged to touch many of the exhibits); habitats housing live reptiles, amphibians, and butterflies; several active research laboratories; colossal dinosaur and whale skeletons frozen in time under the airy atrium; and an observational veterinary clinic are just a few thrilling highlights. Even the exterior of the building is grandiose, adorned with a sleek, 70-foot globe that doubles as a multistory theater inside the museum.

11 W Jones St., (919) 707-9800
naturalsciences.org

CELEBRATE DIVERSITY AND EQUALITY
AT OUT! RALEIGH PRIDE

In addition to providing community outreach, support, and resources, the LGBT Center of Raleigh also hosts Out! Raleigh Pride, a smashing good time of a festival to celebrate inclusiveness and diversity. It happens annually for a day on and around Fayetteville Street, and participants come dressed down, dressed up, holding flags, wearing face paint, blending in, standing out, and enthusiastic to be part of the scene. An enriching mix of live performers takes the stage in the form of bands, DJs, improv teams, dancers, drag entertainers, and a cappella groups. This free festival includes ample food and beverage trucks and vendors, and a KidsZone. As a member, friend, or ally of the LGBT community in Raleigh, don't miss this opportunity to engage with culture and diversity.

(919) 832-4484
lgbtcenterofraleigh.com

TOUR THE EARLIEST HOME OF THE NC LEGISLATURE
AT THE NORTH CAROLINA STATE CAPITOL

At the end of Fayetteville Street, our state capitol building stands as a sturdy reminder of Raleigh's past success and future potential. Surrounded by rippling lawns and impressive, larger-than-life monuments, the columned, massive building in the Greek Revival style of architecture is a National Historic Landmark and current home to the offices of the North Carolina governor. Step inside the cool, stone interior for a self-guided tour. The airy, central rotunda houses a statue of George Washington, along with other busts of important historical figures. Visit the House and Senate chambers, designed in a classical style similar to the building's facade. At night, the exterior of the building is awash in golden light, the perfect focal point for an evening stroll.

1 E Edenton St., (919) 733-4994
historicsites.nc.gov/all-sites/n-c-state-capitol

TIP

For more evening eye candy, amble a couple of blocks down the road to North Blount Street for a glimpse of the breathtaking North Carolina Executive Mansion, a real dazzler when draped in lights for the holidays.

TOUR THE HOME
OF AN INFLUENTIAL RALEIGH DOCTOR AND LEADER AT THE POPE HOUSE MUSEUM

In 1901, Dr. Manassa Thomas Pope built a home boldly ahead of its time, with advanced features like running water in the kitchen, electric fixtures, and a telephone. Many of the original artifacts from Dr. Pope's life, such as his books, medicine bag, and voter registration card, remain on display in the house, offering a window into the life of a prominent African American physician at the turn of the 20th century. Now surrounded by a bustling downtown and modern skyscrapers, the Pope House is a humble reminder of Raleigh's rich history. Stop in at the only African American house museum in the state to learn about Dr. Pope, the lone Black candidate to run for mayor of a Southern capital during the Jim Crow era.

511 S Wilmington St., (919) 996-2220
raleighnc.gov/parks/content/precrecreation/articles/hrmpope.html

TREAT YOURSELF TO ULTIMATE LUXURY
AT THE UMSTEAD HOTEL AND SPA

Whether lodging as an area visitor or indulging in a "staycation," the Umstead is a dream of a retreat, having earned the most prestigious accolades available in the world. The hotel, spa, and restaurant, Herons, all received a five-star rating from Forbes Travel Guide, making it one of the few establishments on planet Earth to score this trifecta. The American Automobile Association (AAA) has deemed it a Five-Diamond property, and *Condé Nast Traveler* named it the third-best hotel in the United States. On paper, it's staggering; in person, it's stunning. Acres of natural forests and a private pond surround sleek architecture in a sanctuary of serenity. For an unparalleled culinary escapade, luxuriate in chef Steven Devereaux Greene's "Art Tour," an eight-course tasting presentation inspired by the hotel's private art collection. Splendor awaits.

100 Woodland Pond Dr., (919) 447-4000
theumstead.com

COMBINE YOUR PASSIONS
AT VITA VITE

Art + wine. Was ever there such a match made in heaven? With two locations in Raleigh, Vita Vite offers double the opportunity for a marriage of the two. Furnished like a cozy living room, Vita Vite is part wine bar, part art gallery, part small-plate kitchen, all under one roof. At each location, there is ample, plush seating both inside and outside for a supremely relaxing atmosphere. Vita Vite Midtown even has an upper-level balcony, affording a lovely panoramic view of Midtown Park. Works by Southern artists hang among the decor in each space, yours for the taking (well, buying) if a piece strikes your fancy. Given the congenial nature of the gallery, you can more realistically picture how the artwork would complement your own abode.

Vita Vite Downtown
313 W Hargett St., (919) 803-3156

Vita Vite Midtown
200 Park Drive at North Hills Street, #130, (919) 322-0649

vitaviteraleigh.com

CHASE DOWN THE NEW YEAR
AT WRAL FIRST NIGHT RALEIGH

We'll take a cup o' kindness yet for auld lang syne! As the final hours of the year rush by, downtown Raleigh transforms into a full-blown carnival. The festivities begin in the afternoon with a family friendly Children's Celebration. The evening heats up with live performances peppered throughout the city blocks, plenty of food offerings, and a Ferris wheel. Take your pick of dancing, magic, comedy, music, or all of the above as you make your way toward Fayetteville Street for the finale. A live band on the City Plaza Main Stage rings in the new year, while the 10-foot-tall acorn sculpture (commissioned for the City of Oaks, get it?) marks the occasion with a ball drop as fireworks boom in the background.

(919) 832-8699
artsplosure.org/events/#first-night-banner

SHOPPING AND FASHION

SUPPORT LOCAL CREATORS
AT BAYLEAF MARKET

An unassuming yet exceedingly charming roadside shop with a killer front porch, Bayleaf Market is the ultimate rustic home for all things North Carolina. Inside the cozy space, one-of-a-kind creations showcase the talent and creativity of our local artists. Small-batch pottery, hand-painted cards, leather goods, soaps, jewelry, wood furniture, knits, paintings, and provisions are crafted by Raleigh-based creators, using local resources with themes often inspired by North Carolina culture. With a constantly rotating inventory, Bayleaf Market is a small but mighty leader in community-focused art and entrepreneurship, frequently offering local, fresh produce, North Carolina seafood, and meats from area farms alongside its gifts and accessories. There's something heartwarming about knowing that the proceeds from your purchase are headed to a neighbor just down the road.

11723 Six Forks Rd., (984) 810-3174
bayleafmarketraleigh.com

FIND THE PERFECT
SOMETHING SOUVENIR
AT DECO RALEIGH

In the heart of downtown, DECO is eclectic, nostalgic, and unapologetically Raleigh-centric. DECO's success over the past decade is a testament to the owners' knowing vision that Raleigh is a city of enthusiastic local-product lovers. The funky, geometric facade is the tip of the iceberg compared with the explosion of creativity that awaits inside. After combining the original gift shop with DECO Home, an updated, expansive space was born, positively spilling with quirky and clever gifts, gadgets, artwork, and every kind of charming, intriguing, or functional accessory in between. Many products feature hilariously witty graphics with a splash of Raleigh flavor. Stop in for a souvenir from the City of Oaks or amp up your collection of hometown accoutrements in this unique, fun-loving shop.

207 S Salisbury St., (919) 828-5484
decoraleigh.com

SHOP HIS AND HERS BOUTIQUES
AT EDGE OF URGE
AND UNLIKELY PROFESSIONALS

These sibling boutiques were founded with the kind of hometown hero spirit that makes Raleigh feel at once like a friendly neighborhood and an exciting hub. The initiative to curate unique and independently crafted goods began with a tiny maker space in Wilmington and has taken Raleigh by storm with this duo of distinctive boutiques. The elder child, Edge of Urge, boasts a large swath of apparel, accessories, gifts, and art from North Carolina creators, purposefully selected with the customers in mind. Sink into "Renew," the self-care corner, with products dedicated to well-being and restoration. Unlikely Professionals, which is grittier, more masculine, and provisioned with a full wine and beer bar, came as an expansion of Edge of Urge's menswear line. Shop one, shop both, always find something unique.

Edge of Urge
215 E Franklin St., #110, (919) 827-4000
edgeofurge.com

Unlikely Professionals
212 E Franklin St., (919) 827-4000
unlikelyprofessionals.com

FIND INSPIRATION FROM SUCCESS STORIES
AT THE FLOURISH MARKET

Raleigh as a city is in the business of doing good, thanks to entrepreneurs like Emily Grey. She started her market on wheels as a traveling fashion truck, found hugely enthusiastic patronage, and eventually settled the shop at its permanent residence in the Warehouse District. It's a fitting success story for the merchandise sold at Flourish. Every single product, from clothing to leather goods and jewelry to accessories, supports social and community revitalization. Many of the craftswomen behind the beautiful and stylish inventory have started afresh with their businesses after surviving sex trafficking, persecution, famine, HIV, and other debilitating circumstances. The boutique is brimming with bold messages ("I will choose to flourish") and stories of perseverance that you can't help but feel inspired to support and join.

307 W Martin St., (984) 202-5035
theflourishmarket.com

WIND THROUGH
A EUROPEAN ESCAPE
AT LAFAYETTE VILLAGE

Designed to resemble a quaint European village, this charming hamlet, complete with its own little Eiffel Tower, is postcard-adorable and populated with divine restaurants and unique shopping. While the aesthetic breathes French allure, the restaurants are positively cosmopolitan in their diversity. Try locally roasted java at Jubala (considered some of the best in Raleigh), authentic Mexican cuisine at Driftwood Cantina, or French classics at Simply Crêpes. With other cuisine-centric retail like the Chocolate Boutique and the Olive Wagon, Lafayette Village goes above and beyond to satisfy the fervent foodie. Specialty shops, salons, and boutiques are peppered in along the village streets. Other ways to enjoy the ambience: head to a pop-up weekend market or festival, or spread a blanket on the Lafayette Village lawn.

8450 Honeycutt Rd., (919) 714-7447
lafayettevillageraleigh.com

ENCOUNTER ENDLESS GREENERY AND HOMEGROWN PRODUCTS
AT LOGAN'S GARDEN SHOP

You could be a hobbyist gardener, a professional horticulturist, or simply an admirer of green things that grow, and Logan's would not disappoint. This garden shop, owned and operated by the Logan family since 1965, looks like it sprouted from magic beans. Blooms, shrubs, trees, succulents, vegetables, and herbs line the outdoor space in rows of vibrant life. In addition to the robust outdoor center, the indoor shop features greenhouse flora as well as every accessory under the sun to aid the green thumb. Don't miss the scores of homegrown products like preserves, produce, and sweets, or stop by the in-store Seaboard Café for lunch. Logan's has routinely earned local and national recognition, and it continues to pursue philanthropic programs and partnerships aimed at providing fresh food for families in need.

707 Semart Dr., (919) 828-5337
logantrd.com

CAPTURE QUIRK AND FUNCTIONALITY
AT NOFO @ THE PIG

NOFO is a fusion of the words *North* and *Fourth*, and *at the Pig* refers to its home inside a renovated Piggly Wiggly store. A café, gourmet gift haunt, truffle counter, toy store, and home goods proprietor, it has no shortage of charm. Upstairs, in the shop, you'll find an array of eclectic gifts and goods with everything from jewelry to furniture and kitchenware to books, not to mention mouthwatering seasonal truffles and candies, pantry staples, and grab-and-go meals. Many of NOFO's products, both edible and otherwise, are supplied by local, small-batch artisans. Downstairs, the café is open for lunch and dinner. The pimento cheese and bloody Mary are both a must, frequently and widely praised as the best around.

2014 Fairview Rd., (919) 821-1240
nofo.com

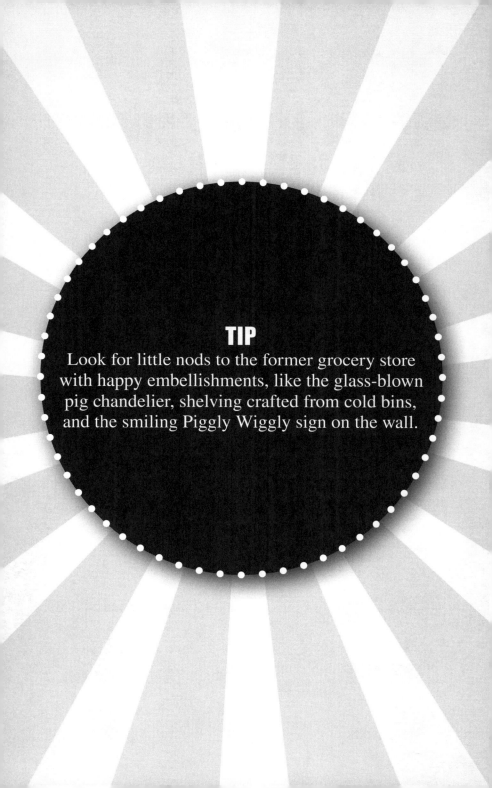

TIP

Look for little nods to the former grocery store with happy embellishments, like the glass-blown pig chandelier, shelving crafted from cold bins, and the smiling Piggly Wiggly sign on the wall.

PICK UP LOCAL PRODUCE
AT THE NORTH CAROLINA STATE
FARMERS MARKET

Agriculture in North Carolina is a powerhouse provider of provisions across the area and nation, and an important cornerstone of state culture. At the Farmers Market, growers and craftspeople bring the farm to you with a bounty of homegrown fare and handmade products. In the open-air farmers' building, pick up fresh, seasonal produce and baked goods. The indoor Market Shoppes is the "old country store" with traditional, North Carolina-born staples like cheeses, preserves, sauces, and marinades. Shop for home and garden furnishings at Market Imports, also on the property, and come hungry for a meal at Market Grill, North Carolina Seafood Restaurant, or State Farmers Market Restaurant. Whether you purchase or peruse, it's a memorable place to feel the fibers of North Carolina tradition in food and lifestyle.

1201 Agriculture St., (919) 733-7417
ncagr.gov/markets/facilities/markets/raleigh

TIP
The North Carolina State Farmers Market is open seven days a week, year-round, excepting Christmas Day.

EXPLORE ENDLESS DINING AND RETAIL
AT NORTH HILLS

In a multi-decade effort to develop and shape Raleigh's Midtown neighborhood, a wildly successful, mixed-use buzzy hub for retail, office, and residential space was born. At the heart is North Hills shopping center, a profusion of diverse dining and merchandising within a pedestrian-friendly, outdoor plaza. You would be hard-pressed to explore it all at once; you'll find everything from favorite chain retailers to local, one-of-a-kind boutiques and other stops, classic and eclectic, like fitness centers, pharmacies, banks, jewelers, salons, spas, and a cinema. Dining, too, is an area of abundance, no matter the occasion: on-the-go options, stay-a-while sit-downs, ritzy presenters, and casual comforts. On the large, central lawn, you can enjoy farmers markets, festivals, live music, and outdoor group fitness classes.

4321 Lassiter Mill Road at North Hills Avenue, (919) 369-4089
visitnorthhills.com/directory/category/shop

TIP
Take advantage of free and plentiful parking, using spaces around the shopping center and in the underground deck.

DISCOVER NEW AND UNIQUE READS
AT QUAIL RIDGE BOOKS

Quail Ridge is an emporium of the written word, a bibliophile's haven, and a local leader in educational engagement. Chain and web vendors have enormous reach but for that reason are often tethered to mainstream media. This independent book store in North Hills fills in the spaces big retailers can't. With a community-driven mission, Quail Ridge is invested in lifting up new writers, seeking out a diverse inventory, and supporting local charities. Plus, you can join its book clubs; attend signings, workshops, and events; listen to its weekly podcast (*Bookin'*); or just spend a quiet afternoon browsing the stacks for staff picks or something entirely unexpected. Since 1984, the readers of Raleigh have relied on Quail Ridge for the thrill of finding their next treasured read.

4209-100 Lassiter Mill Rd., (919) 828-1588
quailridgebooks.com

UPHOLD HIGH ETHICAL JEWELRY STANDARDS
AT QUERCUS STUDIO

Special occasions call for special jewelry. Quercus Studio owner and goldsmith Lauren Ramirez believes that her timeless and beautiful creations should never be marred by poor ethical standards. Inside her workshop and boutique, she handcrafts fine jewelry using only 100 percent post-consumer resources. Fused from carefully selected, recycled metals and reclaimed mined stones from vintage jewelry, treasures at Quercus Studio are sustainable and unique, crafted right there on-site. In addition to featuring gift products created by other artists, the shop also offers private appointments and consultations to flesh out a vision for custom engagement rings and wedding bands, its specialty. Stop by this bright and charming downtown space and make your next piece a one-of-a-kind, ethical purchase.

201 S Salisbury St., (919) 960-1355
quercusraleigh.com

DELVE INTO PRODUCE
FROM THE CITY'S OWN SOIL
AT RALEIGH CITY FARM

Small but robust, Raleigh City Farm, an acre-wide nonprofit nestled among the downtown developments, is a pioneer in community-driven growing and invites you to "dig where you live." In response to the gap that exists in distance and interaction between growers and consumers, Raleigh City Farm is reigniting rendezvous with fresh food. A formerly unoccupied lot, the land has been revitalized like a phoenix from the ashes. On Wednesday afternoons from April through October, show up to shop the harvest of your neighborhood farmers. Compost from the city fuels the soil in a beautiful cycle of waste and reuse. You can also join the Cultivator Club to further support the farm in its effort to share produce with other nonprofits addressing food insecurity.

800 N Blount St., info@raleighcityfarm.org
raleighcityfarm.org

SLIDE INTO YOUR FAVORITE PAIR OF JEANS
AT RALEIGH DENIM
WORKSHOP AND CURATORY

Giorgio Armani said, "Jeans represent democracy in fashion." So, could there be anything more American? Everyone's in search of "a pair of jeans that fit just right": you, me, Zac Brown, and especially Raleigh Denim founders Sarah Yarborough and Victor Lytvinenko. True to its name, their Warehouse District space is the seat of their handmade, small-batch, North Carolina-sourced denim operation (the workshop) and the boutique where you can pick out a perfect pair (the curatory). In addition to selling functional, field-tested clothing, their shop also features other quality products from around the globe under an intriguing ceiling display of thousands of ornate paper airplanes. In unparalleled transparency of process, you can peep through the workshop window to witness the jeansmiths at work, measuring, cutting and stitching, and creating.

319 W Martin St., #100, (919) 917-8969
raleighworkshop.com

WANDER THROUGH AISLES OF INCREDIBLE ECLECTICISM
AT THE RALEIGH MARKET

There are flea markets, and then there are flea markets that are the largest in the state. This is one of the latter. As entrancing as it is functional, this market is a zany mixture of the new and used, modern and vintage, global and homegrown, and pretty much every other conceivable category. Rain or shine, market vendors set up at the North Carolina State Fairgrounds each weekend like a village of curiosities. Food and beverage trucks, as well as farm stands sporting fresh produce, poke in here and there. This purveyor of the practical and peculiar is a collector's paradise and has been recognized by local and national media as one of the best flea markets in the country and a choice treasure trove for antiquing.

4285 Trinity Rd., (919) 839-4560
theraleighmarket.com

BLAST YOUR WAY TO THE PAST
AT RALEIGH VINTAGE

Does your heart belong to another decade? Perhaps your modern wardrobe needs a timeless twist from the past! Raleigh Vintage is an oasis of enduring fashion, featuring clothing and accessories stretching as far back as the 1920s, all the way through present trends. It's a sustainable way to shop, repurposing old garments for an updated look but also inviting a sense of adventure as you journey back through the decades to find highlights of design and style. The antiques of clothing, vintage garments offer an intimate connection to the personalities, ambitions, and lifestyles of past owners and wearers. Become someone else for the day, piece together a zesty wardrobe for your next costume party, or enrich your look with a little piece reminiscent of another era.

18 Glenwood Ave., (919) 348-9310
raleighvintage.com

FURNISH A UNIQUELY YOU SPACE
AT UNION CAMP COLLECTIVE

At Union Camp Collective, experimentation is encouraged, and rules are few and far between. Founder Charlotte Smith says, "I believe you should surround yourself with the things that you love." We complex, idiosyncratic humans sure love a lot of things, so consider this your encouragement for free-rein creativity in the home decor department. Brimming or minimal, colorful or subdued, vintage or modern, there is no "right" way to nest. It's best just to come in person and roam this funky shop for inspiration until you find the perfect piece (or pieces) that is quintessentially "you." Union Camp specializes in antique and unique furniture, as well as home regalia with a spunky flair that just doesn't exist in big-box stores.

(919) 601-9206
unioncampcollective.com

STROLL THE SIDEWALKS
OF YOUR FRIENDLY NEIGHBORHOOD HUB AT VILLAGE DISTRICT

Village District is everything you could want in a shopping center: outdoor walkability, myriad retail, and sustenance on every corner. Even with such diverse offerings, the vibe is more neighborhood-cozy than shopping-frenzy. Charlotte's is a great stop for gifting, and if you're looking to treat the four-legged friend in your life, trot on over to Woof Gang Bakery. For the leaf lover, Tin Roof Teas is worth stopping in just for the trance-inducing aromas. Adventure enthusiasts will delight in Great Outdoor Provision Company, though be warned, you may accidentally depart with enough gear to hike the Appalachian Trail. One of the best times to visit Village District is during the holidays, when colored lights adorn the trees and add a little twinkle of magic to the season.

2034 Cameron St., (919) 821-1350
shopvillagedistrict.com

GOGGLE AT LARGER-THAN-LIFE WHIMSICAL CREATIONS
AT WHEN PIGZ FLY

A lone building in a gravel lot a little north of the city, this local shop is anything but nondescript. It's a drive-by-accidentally, do-a-double-take kind of spectacle. Outside, hundreds of colorful metal sculptures adorn the property like a cast of whimsical characters. Crafted from a plethora of repurposed materials like copper, iron, bottles, cans, cutlery, and garden tools, the artwork is beyond imaginative, morphed into dreamlike, larger-than-life flowers, dinosaurs, insects, machinery replicas, and of course flying pigs. Inside the shop, further whimsy ensues with a colorful, broad selection of home goods, pottery, and provisions crafted by local artists and purveyors. For something magnificent and eye-popping or small and functional, the options are groovy and plentiful.

11125 Six Forks Rd., (919) 235-0250
whenpigzflyshop.com

TAKE CARE OF YOUR PLANT FLEET
AT THE ZEN SUCCULENT

Plant parents rejoice: this charming neighborhood shop has you covered on all fronts, from maintaining your current brood to adding a new member. With their variety, intriguing shapes, and low-maintenance requirements, succulents and cacti contribute a certain sensible liveliness to your space. Like the name suggests, there's a feeling of "ahhhh" when you walk into this vibrant, greenery-shrouded space. Founded and operated by a mother/daughter duo, the ZEN Succulent is a modern mix of urban and earthy, selling one-of-a-kind, hand-assembled terrariums, eccentric and classic planters and containers, books, home decor, self-care products, and myriad other goodies for gardens and greenery. Let your creativity roam free at the DIY terrarium bar or attend an in-store workshop for guidance and inspiration.

Raleigh
208 S Wilmington St., (919) 916-5115

Durham
123 Market St., Ste. B, Durham, (919) 480-1762

thezensucculent.com

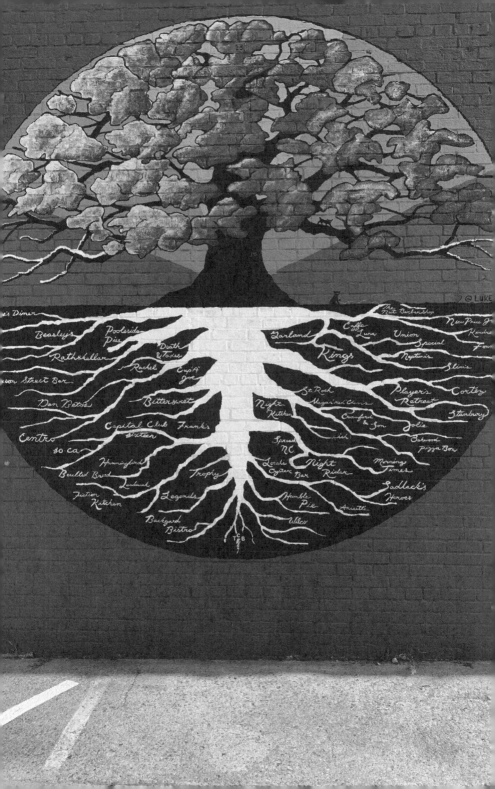

ACTIVITIES
BY SEASON

WINTER

Revel in Elegance at Carolina Ballet, 26

Keep Up with NHL Action with the Carolina Hurricanes, 50

Nestle among the Trees at Koka Booth Amphitheatre, 35

Run, Wolf Down a Dozen Doughnuts, Run Back at the
     Krispy Kreme Challenge, 63

Amp Up Your Holiday Spirit at Meadow Lights, 38

Guffaw and Reflect at Theatre in the Park, 45

Chase Down the New Year at WRAL First Night Raleigh, 101

SPRING

Reimagine Paintings as Floral Arrangements at Art in Bloom, 78

Shop Handmade and Spectate at Artsplosure: The Raleigh Arts Festival, 80

Jam with J. Cole at Dreamville Festival, 30

Appreciate Floral Themes at J. C. Raulston Arboretum, 59

Traipse through Rare Flora at Juniper Level Botanic Garden, 60

Get Your Football Fix at WakeMed Soccer Park, 69

• •

SUGGESTED
ITINERARIES

CAFFEINE AND CONFECTIONS

FERMENTED FAVORITES

• •

EYE CANDY EPICENTERS

FARM-FRESH FOOD

• •

DO GOODERS

FESTIVAL AFICIONADOS

• •

GARDEN GOODNESS

KEEN FOR COMPETITION

• •

KID-FRIENDLY KICKS

• •

OUTDOOR ADVENTURES

RALEIGH ICONS

SEASONAL AND CELEBRATORY

TOURS AND TASTINGS

• •

TUNE TOWN

THROWBACKS

WORLDLY WONDERS

• •

INDEX

• •

• •

• •